M000004984

EDUARDO U. RODRIGUEZ GALVEZ
Coleccionador Industrial

ETHICS
IN PUBLIC ADMINISTRATION

Ethics
in Public Administration

A PHILOSOPHICAL APPROACH

Patrick J. Sheeran

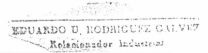
EDUARDO U. RODRIGUEZ GALVEZ
Relacionador Industrial

PRAEGER

Westport, Connecticut
London

Library of Congress Cataloging-in-Publication Data

Sheeran, Patrick J.
    Ethics in public administration : a philosophical approach /
Patrick J. Sheeran.
        p.   cm.
    Includes bibliographical references and index.
    ISBN 0–275–94311–9 (alk. paper)
    1. Public administration—Moral and ethical aspects.   2. Public
administration—United States.   3. Political ethics—United States.
I. Title.
JF1525.E8S45   1993
172′.2—dc20   92–33333

British Library Cataloguing in Publication Data is available.

Copyright © 1993 by Patrick J. Sheeran

All rights reserved. No portion of this book may be
reproduced, by any process or technique, without the
express written consent of the publisher.

Library of Congress Catalog Card Number: 92–33333
ISBN: 0–275–94311–9

First published in 1993

Praeger Publishers, 88 Post Road West, Westport, CT 06881
An imprint of Greenwood Publishing Group, Inc.

Printed in the United States of America

The paper used in this book complies with the
Permanent Paper Standard issued by the National
Information Standards Organization (Z39.48–1984).

10 9 8 7 6 5 4 3 2 1

Every reasonable effort has been made to trace the owners of copyright material in this book, but
in some instances this has proven impossible. The author and publisher will be glad to receive
information leading to more complete acknowledgments in subsequent printings of the book and
in the meantime extend their apologies for any omissions.

To Kathleen, Jenni, Jason, P. J. and Robert Emmet

Contents

Preface

In spite of growing interest in ethics that has occurred over the past ten years, the public is not convinced that there has been much improvement in bureaucratic behavior. This may be because schools of public administration have not uniformly instituted courses on ethics. Although scholars in the field of public administration produce new publications concerning ethics and some schools of public administration offer courses in the subject, there is no uniform approach to developing courses in or the teaching of ethics in schools of public administration. In fact, in some schools ethics is a mandatory course, whereas in other schools it is not even optional. The latter schools maintain that they do not neglect ethics, but rather that they offer it as part of other courses in public administration. In both cases, there is no standard way to teach ethics, nor is there a basic course common to all schools.

Public administration is a complex, diverse and exciting discipline involving theories, paradigms and practices often borrowed from other sciences. Many scholars have bemoaned the fact that public administration has been in a state of chaos for years. Some scholars have questioned whether it is a separate discipline at all. But regardless of these allegations, there is no question about the need for and improvement of courses in public administration.

If public administration itself has an identity crisis, it should not be surprising that ethics for public administrators is undergoing a worse identity crisis. Public administration's treatment of ethics involves many things, including whether to use philosophy as its foundation and, if so, whose philosophy to use. Should the works of Aristotle and St. Thomas Aquinas—involving the existence of a real, external world with objective rules, laws and regulations—be the foundation of this ethics? In other words, is a philosophy of absolutes the foundation of ethics? Or should the philosophy of Plato and the German Idealists dictate the approach? Do we live in a subjective world created by human consciousness, where consciousness dictates reality? Are right and wrong things we *interpret* as such? Are right and wrong relative to every actor? Or maybe there is a combination of both approaches that can help in the teaching of ethics.

Many modern scholars also bemoan the current state of U.S. management, in both the private and the public sectors. The public does not hold public managers in high esteem. They often see them as "faceless functionaries."[1] The Reagan administration, in particular, helped accentuate that view of public managers. But courses in management or administration generally aim to prepare managers *to do things right*. Ethics is the other side of the management coin—its purpose is to prepare managers *to do the right thing*. If there are problems in getting managers to do things right, it should be no surprise that managers also have problems determining what is right. Unfortunately, the public often sees public managers as not competent in either regard. Thus, the purpose of ethics is to help managers determine what is right, and act accordingly.

When I began this work, I told a friend from Cleveland that I was working on a book on ethics in public administration. She replied: "That should be easy. All you need to do is bind together 300 blank pages!" That remark summarizes how the public sees the ethics of people in public service. While there have been many ethical lapses, there are far more devoted, dedicated and ethical public servants.

In teaching courses in public administration, including administrative theory, administrative behavior, management and ethics, I have found that the literature and discussion often lead to a consideration of the meaning of human nature, the nature of man, natural law, the world, and cause and effect. These are philosophical terms that students often have difficulty comprehending. Thus, in addition to providing a foundation for ethics, this book explains the philosophical terminology that other sciences assume students understand.

The main purpose of this book, however, is to provide a philosophical setting for ethics, and to examine what human reason by itself can assess as right and wrong for human beings. Human reason is flawed, and therefore ethics as developed by human reason cannot provide all the answers on what is right and what is wrong. But it can and does ask the questions. Many authors acknowledge that ethics should be grounded in philosophy, and they recognize the difficulties involved in such an approach. Nevertheless, this book attempts such a grounding. In doing so, it acknowledges the impossibility of covering every ethical issue. It covers some issues and applies ethical principles to them. But coverage here is not always comprehensive and, therefore, leaves to others the task of more detailed and practical discussion of ethical issues, particularly as they apply to people in public service.

The word *government* comes from the Latin word, *gubernare*, which means "to steer." There are two views on the purpose and role of government discussed in this book: less government and more government. Regardless of which view is embraced, the role of government is one of steering, not of lording over the citizens. Public servants are agents of the government—they *are* the government as far as the ordinary citizen is concerned. As such, they are responsible for steering courses of action or programs for the common good—just as the captain of a ship steers according to recognized standards of safety and etiquette. Public servants must know what are the standards of safety and etiquette—standards of conduct, as some agencies call them. It does not make too much difference whether these standards are developed by others and coded, or determined by public servants from ordinary common sense. Ethics provides options for both processes. People who like to make laws, rules and regulations should have a thorough knowledge of the principles of ethics to ensure that what they develop is *appropriate and ethical*, not whimsical and opportunistic. Ethics provides guidance on both objective and subjective approaches.

I could not have undertaken this work without support and encouragement from the public administration students and faculty at the University of Southern California and George Mason University. Others who supported my efforts include Dr. Frank Gavin, professor of public administration at the University of Southern California and Johns Hopkins University; Dr. Roger Gilbertson, Rear Admiral, USN, and professor of public administration at Shenandoah University; Dr. Julie Mahler, professor of public administration at George Mason University, and Dr. Deborah McFarlane, professor of public administration at University of New Mexico. I owe all of them a debt of gratitude.

Without the support of my wife, Kathleen, and my family I could not have completed this endeavor. I appreciate their efforts and the sacrifices they made.

Finally, I want to thank Anne Kiefer, editor at Praeger Publishers for her suggestions and recommendations that led to publication of this work.

NOTE

1. Harold Gortner, Julianne Mahler, and Jeanne Bell Nicholson, *Organization Theory: A Public Perspective*, p. 290. Chicago: The Dorsey Press, 1987.

PART I

General Ethics

CHAPTER 1

Status of Ethics in Public Administration

THE CURRENT FOCUS ON ETHICS

Ethics in public service has become a major topic in the United States over the past twenty years. A number of scandals, ranging from the Vietnam War to Watergate and more recently the Iran-Contra affair, has focused public attention on the ethical behavior of public officials and public employees. Ethical problems plagued the Reagan administration during its entire eight years in office. This is somewhat perplexing, since the Reagan administration assumed office emphasizing the importance of family, morals and values, and deemphasizing the role of government and the administrative state. More than 150 political appointees of that administration resigned for unethical behavior during those eight years. The moral failure of so many of these political appointees is noteworthy, since the Reagan administration had such strong support from the Moral Majority, Protestant fundamentalists and evangelicals.[1] The number of ethical violations during the Reagan administration was higher than for any other administration. Yet these ethical lapses may represent only the tip of the iceberg for public administrators.

The Reagan administration was not the only one afflicted by ethical lapses. In every administration at the federal level, scandals have occurred not only among political appointees but also among career civil servants. These scandals continue to occur. Even the conservative Thomas Sowell, an economist and a senior fellow at the Hoover Institution, in May 1992 wrote:

The biggest part of the "public service" sector is government. The scandals here, whether involving money or sex, are too numerous to keep track of. These are the wonderful people who have saddled the average American family with thousands of dollars in losses, just from the savings-and-loan disaster alone, quite aside from what they are saddling unborn generations with through the staggering national debt they have run up.[2]

It is obvious that Sowell was including here more than the executive branch of the federal government—if indeed he intended to include the presidency at all. However, his claim is applicable to the legislative and judicial branches of the federal government, and to state and local governments that have also experienced their fair share of violations.

The American public has not always taken such keen interest in the ethics of public administrators. During the first two hundred years of U.S. history, there was little interest in or focus on ethics. In fact, there was little interest in public administration itself. Richard Stillman points out that administration or "executive leadership was indeed something of a dirty word in the minds of the framers [of the Constitution]."[3]

Gradually, owing to demographic changes from a rural to an urban culture and with the development of new technologies, the public demanded more of government in areas such as transportation, education, community health inspection and the like.[4] With these changes, Stillman claims, the "chinking in" of administration occurred in the United States.[5] The administrative state was not so much created or born; it just gradually happened. This did not result from any great theory or set of theories, such as those that governed administrative states in Europe. It happened "more haphazardly," beginning in the 1880s.[6] Stillman writes: "In the process of this chinking, the development of the American administrative state would always be half-formed or incomplete, at least by comparison to the unified and well-developed European administrative systems."[7]

As public administration became established in the United States, scholars and practitioners began to engage in a lively debate of what constitutes public administration. Stillman concedes that even today public administration suffers from "an identity crisis."[8] He provides several different perceptions of what public administration is.[9] It is a little of this and a little of that, and a little of almost everything. Yet it is a discipline linked inseparably with government and politics, and concerned with the *res publica*—the public or common good.

If there was little interest in public administration in the United States until the late nineteenth century, and it is still unclear what public administration is, it is easy to understand the lack of interest until recently in ethics for public administrators. The ethics dimension of public administration seems to have added to public administration's identity crisis. If it is unclear what public administration is, then ethics for public administrators is even more difficult to define.

The ethical lapses associated with the Reagan administration stirred new interest in ethics for public officials and employees. Some schools of public administration have introduced or upgraded their ethics courses. Public agencies have begun to send representatives to ethics conferences. Books and articles on ethics have appeared, such as *Combatting Corruption: Encouraging Ethics: A Sourcebook for Public Service Ethics*,[9] and *Ethics for Public Managers*.[10] One may wonder if the current interest in ethics for public administrators is long overdue or just a passing fad.

Whether a passing fad or not, the public generally concurs with the late Paul Appleby that public morality should be of a higher calibre than private morality, because public employees carry out the public's trust.[11] The public interest is of greater importance than the private interest. Public officials and public employees take an oath of office to faithfully carry out their duties and responsibilities. Yet in spite of the importance the public gives to ethical conduct and the oath of office, many public servants fail to carry out the public trust. They violate their oaths of office and engage in unethical conduct.

Concerned citizens want to know why there are so many violations of ethics in the public sector. Could it be that public servants do not understand their oath of office? Could it be that they do not know the ethical codes that govern their status as public servants? Could it be that they lack knowledge of the ethical principles that enable them to make correct, discretionary decisions? Or could it be that people come to public service from the private sector or professions where there are different—or no—codes of ethics? Appleby acknowledges these difficulties: "The problems of morality press hard and often upon individual public administrators." He adds that some public administrators "have only rudimentary awareness of their peculiarly public responsibilities."[12]

PROBLEMS OF ETHICS IN PUBLIC ADMINISTRATION

Many scholars note that schools of public administration have long neglected courses in ethics. And the current courses in ethics do not satisfy these writers. This is not new. In 1976, Susan Wakefield noted that students preparing for careers in public administration are "in the education system to gain the tools they will need to be effective in their future careers. If a foundation of ethics is neglected, a significant need will be overlooked.

Educators should be willing to assume responsibility for this segment of total education."[13] Wakefield also stated that only "a limited number of people" destined for public service have access to public administration curricula. This situation is even more applicable to curricula in ethics.

Subsequent writers continue to criticize schools of public administration for offering either no ethics courses or only poorly developed ones. But John Rohr[14] and Terry Cooper,[15] while recognizing the importance of teaching ethics in schools of public administration, see insurmountable problems in developing these courses. Writers generally concur that the roots of ethics are the major problem in developing these courses. Should the courses be based on classical ethics, rooted in philosophy, or should they have other roots? Rohr thinks it difficult to do justice to ethics if classical or political ethics (as he calls it) is not the foundation. Yet this situation creates a dilemma: If ethics is derived from philosophy, philosophy will likely be shortchanged owing to a heavy courseload for public administration students. On the other hand, if schools offer no courses in philosophy, or only "a smattering of philosophy," the students are shortchanged. He writes:

But I do not think we can prudently demand *extensive* philosophical investigations for public administration students after they have started their professional studies. To settle for a smattering of political philosophy as part of a course in ethics would not be fair either to the students or to philosophy itself. For this reason we must look elsewhere for the *foundation* of ethics.[16]

Rohr does not completely reject philosophy as the foundation for an ethics course, but he thinks that it is expecting too much of public administration students to study philosophy, since there are so many public administration courses that students must take. With an academic background in both philosophy and theology, Rohr has outstanding qualifications to write on ethics grounded in philosophy. Yet he develops an ethical foundation for bureaucrats based on the U.S. Constitution and on opinions of the U.S. Supreme Court. Rohr writes:

The best educated means of preparing bureaucrats to fulfill this obligation [an oath to uphold the Constitution] is to use Supreme Court opinions on salient regime values to encourage them to reflect on how these values might best influence their decision making as persons who govern.[17]

According to Rohr, then, the best approach is to use Supreme Court opinions on salient regime values, encouraging public servants to consider how these values best influence their decision making. *Regime values* are those of the political entity brought into existence by the creation of the U.S. Constitution. Rohr believes that regime values derived from studies of Supreme Court opinions reflect the public interest or the salient values of society.

It is true that most issues that come before the U.S. Supreme Court produce concurring and dissenting opinions, suggesting that people can interpret the same principle or issue differently. But opinions of the Supreme Court nevertheless result in one decision that public follows until the Court or the legislature changes or reverses it. The public does not have the latitude of following a minority or dissent opinion, although minority opinions nearly always reflect the values and viewpoints of certain segments of society. To that extent, Rohr's approach to ethics has merit.

While public administrators can make ethical decisions by studying opinions of the Supreme Court, these opinions are often tedious and boring. Divergent opinions may provide a framework for decision making, but not necessarily for making the right decisions, which is the core of ethics. While denying that his approach is legalistic, Rohr does not specifically address the more fundamental question: what are the roots of the U.S. Constitution?

Rohr's reliance on the Supreme Court to guide public administrators in discretionary administrative decisions may be useful in the United States. But it is unlikely that these opinions will be helpful to public administrators in other countries. Furthermore, if there were no U.S. Constitution or Supreme Court opinions, on what would public administrators rely for moral guidance? This same criticism is applicable to Immanuel Kant's argument, which claimed that obedience to law through application of the so-called Categorical Imperative made human actions ethical. Apparently something above and beyond the U.S. Constitution and the opinions of the Supreme Court is needed to guide the ethics of public administrators.

Katherine Denhardt acknowledges that ethics has its roots in philosophy, but she shies away from declaring ethics as a branch of philosophy, to be the basis for courses in ethics for public administration. She writes:

The field [public administration] has failed to take advantage of the philosophical traditions that should be underpinnings of any study or the application of ethics. These philosophical traditions include both *ethics as a branch of philosophy* (which deals with how to identify, deliberate, and resolve ethical problems), and *political philosophy* (which has much to say to current public administration about the appropriate roles, behaviors, and values of administrators). Not only would the further development of the philosophical traditions be *helpful* to the field, but it is also *necessary* in that by focusing only on the current state of public administration the field risks developing a narrowly interpreted, self-serving ethic which will neither survive the test of time nor serve the public interest. Therefore, a second objective of this book is to delineate the place of philosophy in administrative ethics, though it will be left to other works yet to come to fully develop this dimension.[18]

Other authors think that classical ethics is outdated, that the principles developed by human reason and related somewhat to theology are outmoded and no longer workable, particularly for people working in the public sector. What they suggest, and what practice frequently bears out, is a so-called ethical principle that might be termed the "done thing." Adolescents are great advocates of this principle: "Everybody is doing it." The claim that everyone is doing something does not always mean that everyone *is* actually doing it; and if everyone is doing it, that does not necessarily mean that the done thing is right. There must be a criterion for morality (what is right or wrong) other than the "done thing."

Business writers such as Peter Drucker, who make no distinction between public and private administration, deny that there is a separate ethics for business. By implication, public administrators do not need a separate code of ethics. Drucker writes: "But there is neither a separate ethics of business, nor is there one needed."[19] According to Drucker, the only ethics needed for all professionals is contained in the Hippocratic oath *"primum non nocere"* ("above all, not knowingly to do harm"). This oath contains a general ethical principle that, as further discussion in this work will show, is derived from the principles of natural law and is addressed in classical ethics.

The distinction between morality and legality is a fundamental problem confronting students of ethics. Professor Jerry Harvey at George Washington University in Washington, D.C., who has successfully integrated ethics with courses in management, has stated that, in the United States, "it is often illegal to be moral, truthful, assume responsibility, be ethical."[20] In Harvey's most recent film, *The Asoh Defense: Managing Blame and Forgiveness*, Japanese airline pilot Captain Asoh safely lands an aircraft short of the runway, but in San Francisco Bay. At the beginning of the investigation to determine what happened, Captain Asoh tells the investigators: "As you Americans say, Captain Asoh screw up!" This is admitting pilot error, assuming responsibility and blame. He tells the truth. But telling the truth may have consequences in terms of legal liability for damages. By telling the truth—being moral—Captain Asoh may run the risk of acting illegally, to the extent that he may have exposed his organization to potential liabilities.[21]

Others undoubtedly may say that it is sometimes immoral to be legal. This claim is frequently made by people in the pro-life movement. They ignore current laws that make abortion legal in the United States, and engage in unauthorized protests, sit-ins and even bombings of abortion facilities. They argue that laws permitting legal abortion are immoral in themselves, and that citizens should not obey them—to obey these "immoral" laws is immoral.

In the last century, Alexis de Tocqueville wrote that, in America, every great question in the society becomes a legal one.[22] If he were alive today, he probably would not confine his observation to the great questions, but include the many minor questions that now reach the Supreme Court. In theory at least, morality and legality in *an ideal world* should be the same. As later discussion in this book shows, legality and morality should overlap, but sometimes they do not. Whatever is moral is not always legal, and whatever is legal may not always be moral. Some writers tend to apply only legal principles to human actions, while others ignore some positive laws. Later discussion of these issues also will show that these behaviors or practices may both be unethical.

Terry Cooper has claimed that ethics is a private matter.[23] In a pluralist society, where people's religion, morals and values differ, it is difficult to teach ethics without also teaching a particular viewpoint or offending those whose views differ. Akin to this is the connection between ethics and religion. Some people identify religion with ethics, and vice versa. Later discussion in this book will show that this identification is unfortunate. Although religion may—and often does—support ethics, the process of deriving ethical principles is quite different from that of theology. Theology relies on divine revelation contained mostly in the Bible, whereas ethics relies on human reason *alone* to develop principles applicable to all people. So ethics is a science that offers general principles governing human behavior, applicable to all human beings. These general principles are developed by human reason, so they are limited because human reason is limited in the extent to which it can discover hidden laws or principles. Undoubtedly, religion clarifies ethics. However, this work will make no effort to supplement ethics with principles or teachings from religion.

APPROACHES TO ETHICS

There are two main approaches to the teaching of ethics. These can influence human behavior in different ways—in fact, in opposite behaviors for the same action, in the same circumstances, by different people. The two approaches are the objectivist, and the interpretivist or subjectivist.

The *objectivist approach* is also known as deontological theory. Advocates of this theory look for objective, ultimate or absolute standards or criteria for assessing the morality (rightness or wrongness) of human actions. The *interpretivist approach* is often called teleological theory. Subscribers to this theory offer no absolute standards for assessing right and wrong. The individual's judgment in particular, unique cases constitutes the only criterion for what is right and what is wrong. In reality, this is "situation ethics," whereby the situation dictates what a person should or should not do and the result is *the right or ethical decision*. The teleological approach considers only the consequences of human actions and makes judgment on these consequences. There are no rules, laws or regulations to help in judging the consequences.

The two approaches are based on theories in other branches of philosophy, particularly ontology and epistemology. The objectivist theory maintains that there is a real, objective world external to human consciousness. There also are real laws and standards that govern everything, including human behavior. The interpretivist theory maintains that there is no real, physical world external to human consciousness. Instead, our consciousness creates the world—the world inasfar as it exists is a product of human consciousness. Burrell and Morgan summarize interpretivism this way: "The external world is shown to be an artefact of consciousness; phenomena are shown to be willed into existence through intentional acts. Man is shown to live in a world created through consciousness."[24]

Cynthia McSwain and Orion White build on Burrell and Morgan's description of interpretivism in general to apply the paradigm to ethics. They say that as consciousness develops in a person from childhood, an ego is developed, which they claim "to consist of and be presented primarily as a set of value commitments. Every ego is in some sense a code of ethics."[25] Based on the McSwain-White theory, one might argue that there are as many codes of ethics as there are people, or that there are as many different and even contradicting codes of ethics as there are people. It is unclear how this approach guides public administrators, particularly in making decisions that their superiors or the public will support. In a bureaucracy replete with rules and regulations and steeped in incrementalism, it is unlikely that the interpretivist approach alone can receive strong support from people in the higher echelons. The interpretivist approach may be easy, but is perhaps too permissive for public administrators. However, it can, as further discussion in this volume will show, be helpful in formulating ethical decisions with other criteria or standards for judging morality.

The conflict between the objectivist and subjectivist approaches, coupled with the difficulties raised by Rohr and Cooper, is a poor excuse for failing to develop and implement ethics courses in schools of public administration. It is important to note that neither the objectivist nor the subjectivist approach will resolve all the difficulties associated with ethics. In fact even together both approaches will not resolve all the ethical problems for public administrators. With the objective of developing a course in ethics for public administrators, this book discusses both approaches, with ethics rooted in philosophy and with a focus on the morality of public administrators. It links ethics with the other branches of philosophy and thus also with teleological theory, also rooted in philosophy. The link between these two theories will be evident when I discuss issues of law and conscience.

This book begins by developing the philosophical "dimension" that Denhardt "left to other works."[26] It marks a departure from Rohr by claiming that ethics, though based on a "smattering of philosophy," is not only important in developing public administration courses in ethics but also in its application to other courses in public administration, including administrative theory, administrative behavior, public policy, evaluation and research.

Courses in philosophy, whether complete or partial, are important for not only public administration but, as Denhardt points out, almost every science. All sciences begin where philosophy ends. Philosophy is the basis for every science. Science relies on and uses the knowledge and practices derived from philosophy. Although many students have not studied philosophy, or have had only a smattering of philosophy, they depend on this subject for supplying the many assumptions that their field or discipline is based on. In short, "Philosophy is the mother of the sciences."

The next two chapters summarize the relevant topics of philosophy, its various branches, and the reliance of one branch on another. They provide that "smattering of philosophy" so as to enrich a study of ethics. Thus, they provide a theoretical framework for the study of ethics.

Many scholars claim that the principles of classical philosophy are outdated and do not apply to the modern world, especially to public administration. It is true that the great philosophers Aristotle and St. Thomas Aquinas did not have access to the discoveries made by modern science. But the "bad science"[27] that they sometimes used does not detract from their scholarly contributions to philosophy. Although their theories may be "old," they are a solid theoretical framework for modern science and ethics. Aristotle and St. Thomas Aquinas never intended that their ideas were complete or the final pronouncement on many issues. But they do serve as a starting point for philosophy and ethics. One can only speculate on what these men's contributions would have been had they experienced modern science and technology.

This study focuses particularly on the writings of St. Thomas Aquinas. The intention is not to overlook Aristotle or many other great philosophers. Since St. Thomas Aquinas broke with Plato but cited and upheld many of Aristotle's teachings, this study also is indirectly based on Aristotle's philosophy. Where "bad science" enters the writings of both philosophers, this study will so note.

It should also be noted that this work provides only a sketch of what philosophy entails. My summary is limited to ontology, epistemology and psychology. It is hoped the principles of logic apply throughout the study.

For those who have studied philosophy, this review will serve as a refresher. For those who have never studied philosophy, the two chapters may seem deep or heavy; however, approach the content as just common sense. These are subjects that you may not have thought of before or thought of only lightly. If you find them too abstract right now, proceed to chapter 4 and return to chapters 2 and 3 later.

Ethics from a deontological perspective provides only the principles—the standards of morality that *ought to be*—and not how people actually act. Thus, ethics is similar to a professional football team's play book. The play book contains the formations or plays the team plans to carry out. But it does not guarantee that the players will actually carry out these plays, owing to a lack of skills or unanticipated skills of the opposition. But ethics from a teleological perspective provides the materials for more sophisticated reflection on the meaning and consequences of human actions. In practice, the two theories come together to help apply general principles to concrete situations, or to reflect broadly on these particular situations. By showing the general principles and presenting conflicting theories, this study shows the difficulties involved in arriving at a consensus on certain moral issues.

The current literature addresses the development and application of an ethics for public administrators. However, it rarely explores the roots of our laws, rules, regulations and standards of conduct. Neither does it discuss the philosophical assumptions that are the basis for the deontological and teleological theories. The approach here is to provide a theoretical framework for developing ethical principles that public administrators can apply to specific situations. By and large, then, this study does not apply ethical principles to routine actions and decisions. Neither does it examine the codes of ethics developed by respectable organizations such as the American Society for Public Administration, the American Medical Society or the American Bar Association. But people involved in developing or revising such codes of ethics might consider the philosophical and theoretical roots of ethics discussed here. Case studies augment and supplement the principles developed here.

NOTES

1. "Whatever Happened to Ethics?" *Time*, May 25, 1987.
2. "So-called 'Greed' vs. Public Service," *Washington Times*, May 17, 1992.
3. Richard J. Stillman, *Preface to Public Administration: A Search for Themes and Direction* (New York: St. Martin's Press, 1991), p. 61.
4. Ibid., pp. 47–48.
5. Ibid., pp. 55–56.
6. Ibid., p. 56.
7. Ibid., p. 56.
8. Ibid., p. vii.
9. William L. Richter, Frances Burke, and Jameson W. Doig, *Combatting Corruption: Encouraging Ethics: A Sourcebook for Public Service Ethics* (Washington, D.C.: American Society for Public Administration, 1990).
10. Harold F. Gortner, *Ethics for Public Managers* (New York: Praeger, 1991).
11. Paul H. Appleby, *Morality and Administration in Democratic Government* (Westport, Conn.: Greenwood Press, 1969), p. 42.
12. Ibid., p. 45.
13. Susan Wakefield, "Ethics and the Public Service: A Case for Individual Responsibility," *Public Administration Review*, November-December 1976, p. 665.
14. John A. Rohr, *Ethics for Bureaucrats* (New York: Marcel Decker, 1978), pp. 65–66.
15. Terry L. Cooper, *The Responsible Administrator* (Port Washington, N.Y.: Associated Faculty Press, 1986), pp. 4–5.
16. Rohr, *Ethics for Bureaucrats*, pp. 65–66.
17. Ibid., p. 5.
18. Katherine G. Denhardt, *The Ethics of Public Service: Resolving Moral Dilemmas in Public Organizations* (Westport, Conn.: Greenwood Press, 1988), pp. vii–viii.
19. Peter F. Drucker, *Management* (New York: Harper and Row, 1974), pp. 368–69.
20. Verbal statement made at a conference.
21. *The Asoh Defense: Managing Blame and Forgiveness*. (Carlsbad, Calif.: CRM Films, 1990).
22. Alexis De Tocqueville, *Democracy in America*, Richard D. Heffner, ed. (New York: New American Library, 1956), p. 126.
23. Cooper, *Responsible Administrator*, p. 5.
24. Gibson Burrell and Gareth Morgan, *Sociological Paradigms and Organizational Analysis* (Portsmouth, N.H.: Heinemann, 1985), p. 233.

25. Cynthia J. McSwain and Orion F. White, "The Case for Lying, Cheating, and Stealing—Personal Development as Ethical Guidance for Managers," *Administration and Society*, *18*, no. 4 (February 1987), p. 419.

26. Denhardt, *Ethics of Public Service*, p. viii.

27. Anton C. Pegis, *Basic Writings of Saint Thomas Aquinas*, Volume One (New York: Random House, 1945), pp. xxxix–liii.

CHAPTER 2

Philosophy and Ontology as the Foundation for Ethics

THE PLACE OF PHILOSOPHY IN PUBLIC ADMINISTRATION

The current literature in public administration sometimes uses terminology unfamiliar to today's students. This is particularly true of courses in administrative theory and administrative behavior. When authors use words such as *ontology* and *epistemology*, they are using philosophical terms.

Authors generally assume that their readers know what these words mean. Many students of public administration, however, have difficulty finding an explanation of these terms and even more difficulty comprehending the distinction between them. In the introduction to their work on the study of organizations, Burrell and Morgan addressed the issue: "We were confronted with problems of ontology and epistemology and other issues which rarely receive consideration within the field of organization studies."[1] These authors used these terms as if students already understood them.

Ontology and epistemology are not only at the foundation of public administration, they are the basis for every other science. Therefore, there is a need to explain the meaning of these terms. In particular, there is a close relationship between ontology and epistemology.

The U.S. Constitution and our political system are both closely tied with philosophy. The framers of the Constitution were well aware of the writings of Aristotle, St. Thomas Aquinas and the contract theorists,

Thomas Hobbes, John Locke and Jean-Jacques Rousseau. These writers were not just politicians; they were also philosophers whose political viewpoints influenced the shape of the Constitution and our political system. In particular, the thinking of these philosophers affected the American public administration system. So a discussion of philosophy is relevant not only to ethics but also to the entire field of public administration.

A DEFINITION OF PHILOSOPHY

Philosophy comes from two Greek words meaning "a love of wisdom." Wisdom is knowledge of all things. Philosophy studies all things. The *American Heritage Dictionary* defines *philosophy* as "love and pursuit of wisdom by intellectual means and moral self-discipline. The investigation of causes and laws underlying reality . . . Inquiry into the nature of things based on logical reasoning rather than empirical methods." *Webster's New Twentieth Century Dictionary* defines *philosophy* as "the ultimate science which aims at an explanation of all phenomena by ultimate causes; the knowledge of phenomena as explained by, and resolved into, ultimate causes and reasons, powers and laws."

These two definitions are quite similar and lead to the following definition: Philosophy is the science that relies solely on human reason to figure out the final or ultimate cause of anything and everything. Things in general or beings, therefore, are the area of inquiry for the science of philosophy. The word *thing* is the most basic and primitive term in our vocabulary. Philosophy focuses on discovering what constitutes the nature of a particular thing—what is its essence, what are its causes and its relationships with other things. It is the science that tries to delve as deep as the human mind can into the nature, purpose and cause of things. Philosophy is the starting point for every science, including public administration. It provides students in every discipline with a fundamental grasp of that discipline by clarifying what is taken for granted.

Philosophy relies solely on the power of the human intellect to investigate the nature of things and their causes. Religion or empirical methods are not part of the methodology. But since human reason is far from perfect, there are limits to the findings and conclusions that can be derived from philosophy. Also, different schools of philosophical thought have emerged because of these limitations of the human intellect. Philosophy, therefore, does *not* provide complete answers to all questions raised by the human mind; and sometimes it provides different and even diametrically opposed views of these questions.

THE DIVISIONS AND BRANCHES OF PHILOSOPHY

Philosophy has two main divisions: speculative (or metaphysics) and general (or practical). *Speculative philosophy* provides knowledge of a subject or area for the sake of knowledge. It attempts to discover ultimate truths about the universe and everything in it. *Practical philosophy* provides knowledge to be used or applied in concrete actions or situations. It leads to action after knowledge has been acquired.

Within these two main divisions are eight closely interrelated and interdependent branches or subject areas, as Figure 1 shows. Speculative philosophy has two areas of interest: general and special. General philosophy studies all beings in general, including their existence and essence

FIGURE 1
Branches of Philosophy

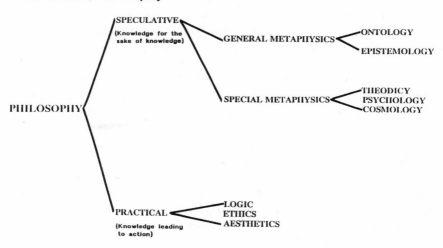

(ontology), and how we acquire knowledge of these things (epistemology). Special philosophy further breaks down the "all things in general" as studied in ontology into three specific categories: matter, studied in cosmology; human beings, studied in psychology, and the supreme being, studied in theodicy.

Practical philosophy involves three practical sciences: logic, which enables human beings to think correctly; ethics, which enables human beings to act or behave correctly; and aesthetics, which enables people to make things beautiful.

HISTORY OF PHILOSOPHY

Over the centuries, philosophy as an area of inquiry has had its vicis-
situdes. At some times, some branches of philosophy flourished more than
others. During other eras, scholars neglected philosophy entirely. Nevertheless, from earliest times, people have sought to understand the meaning
and nature of things around them. At first, the most prominent things were
the earth and the planets. They expressed wonder at these things. Wonder
is the beginning of philosophy.

The ancient Greek philosophers, in response to this wonderment and
curiosity, began to study the universe, desiring to know more about its
constituent elements. During this period the science of cosmology was
dominant.

The Greek philosopher Thales claimed that everything is made of water.
Another Greek philosopher said that air constitutes everything because
nothing can live without air. Democritus held that atoms are the basis of
everything: human beings, animals, and the earth are combinations of
different kinds of atoms, and it is the combination of atoms that makes one
species different from another—as, for example, a human being is different from a tree. Subsequently, Epicurus subscribed to this theory,
thereafter known as Epicureanism. The basis for Epicureanism is materialism—that is, matter constitutes everything. In the sixteenth century,
Thomas Hobbes advanced this theory by claiming that matter and motion
constitute all things. Advocates of Epicureanism made cosmology the
dominant branch of philosophy.

Upon reflecting on these paradigms, another group of philosophers,
the Sophists, concluded that people know nothing! However, this
theory marked the beginning of the philosophical focus on human
beings, as opposed to the earth and heavens. It marked a shift in
emphasis from cosmology to epistemology, ontology, psychology,
ethics and logic.

The Greek philosopher Socrates was the first to concentrate on humans
as an area of inquiry. He emphasized the importance of ideas and the
necessity of having correct ideas. He addressed such issues as people's
knowledge—where and how it is acquired—and laid down the first
scientific standards of ethics governing behavior. His approach resulted in
the emergence of epistemology and ethics.

One of Socrates's most prominent students was Plato. He, too, began
with the notion of ideas, thus confining himself to epistemological and
ontological approaches. He concluded that there exists another world
above and beyond the world we see before us—a world that is above our

powers of sense, which he called a "suprasensible world." Ideas exist in that suprasensible world just as human beings exist in the everyday world. He claimed that people's souls before they inhabited their bodies existed in this suprasensible world of ideas, and it was in this world that these souls obtained all the ideas people now have. This is the theory of *innate ideas*. Plato claimed that we are born with all our concepts and ideas. René Descartes advanced this theory in the seventeenth century, as did Antonio Rosmini in the nineteenth century.[2] Plato concluded that the world in which people live is not the real world; rather, the real world is the world of suprasensible ideas. This is the beginning of the subjectivist or interpretivist paradigm. It is the Platonic school of philosophy.[3]

Plato taught the great philosopher Aristotle, who refuted Plato's theory of a suprasensible world. Aristotle philosophized that all human knowledge begins with the five senses—sight, hearing, smell, taste and touch. But besides the five senses, people have an intellect. The intellect enables people to peel away from knowledge gained through the senses to identify individual characteristics and render the knowledge abstract and universal. It is the intellect, then, that has the capacity to formulate universal ideas, as opposed to Plato's theory of a suprasensible world of ideas.

Aristotle also expounded the doctrine of potency and action as well as the doctrine of change. He developed the teaching of the four causes of change—material, formal, efficient and final—that will be explored later in this chapter in relation to ontology. Finally, it was Aristotle who taught that man is composed of two principles—a body and a soul—which are joined together.[4]

Aristotle's approach combined epistemology, ontology and psychology. He was the founder of the peripatetic school of philosophy, often called empiricism, although in the seventeenth century John Locke modified this theory by discarding the role of the human intellect in the search for knowledge. Following Aristotle, the Platonic school existed side by side with the peripatetic school.

The arrival of Christianity added a new dimension to philosophy, as philosophers attempted to link theology and philosophy. Two renowned philosophers during the first five centuries A.D. include St. Ambrose and St. Augustine. This period, known as the patristic era, witnessed the dissolution of the Roman Empire. It was not a time conducive to the study of philosophy. But beginning with the coronation of Charlemagne in A.D. 800, there was an era of peace with emphasis on education. The Christian monks, particularly the Irish monks, had preserved the works of former philosophers, so that philosophers such as St. Alexander the Great and St. Bonaventure could reintroduce the study of philosophy.

It was, however, St. Thomas Aquinas in the thirteenth century who perhaps more than any other scholar since Aristotle contributed most to modern philosophy. His most famous contribution was the *Summa Theologica*, which is a combination of both philosophy and theology. It was Aquinas who mapped out for all time the distinction and the relationships between philosophy and theology. Going back to the Greek philosophers, he shaped the known philosophical theories into one system. In particular, he added to ontology and epistemology certain doctrines, including the theory of moderate realism, the unity of substantial form in every individual, the doctrine of subsistent forms and the real distinction between the soul and its faculties.[5]

The Renaissance turned scholars' minds toward a study of the classics and away from philosophy. The Reformation also caused serious doubts about the nature of people and particularly about the acquisition of knowledge. But it was not until René Descartes in the seventeenth century that modern philosophy began. Descartes, a mathematician, approached the study of philosophy that paralleled Euclid. He concentrated particularly on ontology and epistemology, with some initial success. About the same time, Thomas Hobbes, John Locke and Jean-Jacques Rousseau were focusing on philosophy, particularly on the nature of human beings, society and the state. Ontology and epistemology were of great interest.

As noted, Hobbes subscribed to Epicureanism, emphasizing that matter and motion constitute everything. Locke, on the other hand, subscribed to the basic philosophy of Aristotle and became a great advocate of empiricism. He claimed that humans were born with a *tabula rasa* and that we acquire all knowledge through the senses alone. He denied any real difference between concept and sense image. A concept, according to Locke, is another form of sensation. Locke's version of empiricism held that the only knowledge we have is sense knowledge, and the only things we can know are what we learn through the five senses; the intellect is not involved in the acquisition of knowledge. This view signified a departure from Aristotle, who maintained that the intellect plays a vital role in acquiring knowledge. There is further exploration of this theory in the discussion of epistemology later in this chapter.

It was not until the eighteenth century that the German idealist Immanuel Kant brought the study of epistemology to the forefront, a position it has continued to hold. During this period, Irish philosopher Bishop George Berkeley became an ardent advocate of solipsism, or the Platonic school of philosophy, and denied the existence of a real physical world. In the nineteenth century, philosophers such as Hegel, Ingel and Marx also contributed significantly to modern philosophy.

In the twentieth century, theorists such as Husserl, Schutz, Lukacs, Gramasci and the Frankfurt school, especially Habermas and Marcuse, further expanded the German idealist philosophy of Hegel and that of Marx as a young man.[6] Burrell and Morgan, although writing about organizations primarily from a sociological perspective, broadened their approach to include "many aspects of philosophy and social theory in general."[7] In doing so, they provide an excellent overview of the philosophical issues and related problems arising from ontology and epistemology. In particular, they show that the writings of authors identified with the Frankfurt school have a philosophical basis and their opinions or theories have a corresponding application to organizational life.

Burrell and Morgan have also provided the foundation for the two schools of thought on ethics—the deontological and the teleological approaches. But before further exploring these, it is useful to examine the main branches of philosophy, particularly ontology, epistemology and psychology, that significantly influence both ethics and public administration.

ONTOLOGY

It amazes most students when they hear that some philosophers deny the existence or reality of an external world. It sounds ridiculous and crazy to claim that the desk at which I sit or the student next to me in class is not real—at best creations of my mind or radio waves. It is even harder to claim that if I kick a rock, I have not hit a real object, especially since my foot is enduring pain. But there is a school of thought that holds just that. And these philosophers are not crazy people!

Ontology is the philosophical science that studies being as common to all things or objects. Following the methodology of philosophy, it uses unaided human reason to study beings. The term *being* is understood in its broadest sense, and applies to both human beings and inanimate objects. It is the simplest of notions, the first idea human beings acquire, the most indeterminate notion in that it can be applied to everything, including human beings, animals, the world and its contents. Ontology uses the word *being* in these cases analogously—that is, in not exactly the same meaning because clearly there are differences between *being* applied to a person and being applied to an animal or a tree. The word is also the most abstract of ideas because it is smallest in connotation and broadest in denotation. Ontology is, therefore, the starting point and basic subject of philosophy.

In essence, ontology contains three parts. The first addresses the meaning of *being*; the second deals with the ten categories of being; the third investigates the causes of being.

The Meaning and Types of Being

Orthodox or traditional ontology defines *being* as anything that exists or can exist. It distinguishes among different types or categories of beings, such as real beings that exist independently of our thoughts and ideal beings that connote the presence of a known object within the knowing mind. According to this distinction, *real* beings exist outside and independently of the human mind. They exist whether the human mind is thinking about them or not.

Ideal beings, strictly according to the traditional school, are products of the union between the knowing mind and a real object in the external world. Real beings, therefore, cause ideal beings to exist. The presence of a known object within the human mind is an ideal being.

But there are other schools of thought on this notion of the ideal being. One school of philosophers, the phenomenologists, have attempted to suspend consideration of objectivity and subjectivity of phenomena, or the distinction between real and ideal beings, to come to a better understanding of the meaning of *being* in itself. Other philosophers have broadened the distinction of ideal beings to mean that the human mind creates the products called "real"—the human mind creates the world as we know it. This view has its roots in the Platonic theory. It is the extreme phenomenological theory or solipsism propounded by Bishop Berkeley, who maintained that a real, external world may not exist and the only reality may be the spirit and the supreme being.[8]

Berkeley's theory of solipsism seems to confuse ideal beings with a third category of beings, which ontology calls *logical beings*. Logical beings have no existence or being at all except insofar as they are products of thought. For example, a square circle exists only in the mind and is clearly a creation of the mind. Another example is the sentence "John is a student." The relationship between the subject and predicate is a logical being. *John* and *student* both exist, but the sentence, "John is a student," exists only in the human mind and is a logical being. Logical beings exist nowhere except in the human mind.

Ontology focuses on the supreme principles of being. *Principle* means "that from which something proceeds in any form." For example, fire is the principle of heat. There are four supreme principles applicable to being: (1) the principle of identity; (2) the principle of contradiction; (3) the principle of excluded middle; and (4) the principle of sufficient reason. These four principles have roots in both ontology and logic.

The principle of identity means simply that everything is what it is and not something else, as, for example, a man is a man and not a tree. We use the principle of identity in every affirmative statement we make. The principle of contradiction is also simple. It arises from the comparison between being and nothing. When we compare the two ideas, being and nothing, clearly one cannot be the other. It is impossible for a thing to be and not to be simultaneously. The principle of excluded middle arises again from a comparison between being and nothing—there is no middle ground between these two ideas, being and nothing. The principle of sufficient reason means that whatever reality a being has, it must owe that reality to itself or, if not, depend on something else for it. In the first case, the being has sufficient reason for its reality in itself. In the second case, sufficient reason for its reality lies in something else. Classical ontology uses these four principles to establish the existence of a real, physical world external to the human mind and existing independently of the human mind.

When a being develops a relationship with a human mind or intellect, the notion of ontological truth arises. Ontological truth means the conformity of a thing (being) to thought. It means that a particular object corresponds to the thought of that object, which a person has in his or her mind. Where do these ideas or ideal types in the human mind come from? Plato claimed that human beings were born with them and therefore real objects do not necessarily exist. Things have ontological truth only when a person has formed mental concepts or images of those particular types of things.[9] According to Aristotle and the empirical school, people are not born with these concepts so they must come from experience, through observation and through learning. This school argues that things exist whether or not people have or ever had thoughts about them. It argues that even before human minds existed, these things have an ontological reality—they already exist independently of and external to human minds.[10] But according to some empiricists such as John Locke, human beings cannot know the essence of these objects, nor can they subscribe the notions of cause and effect to them.[11]

The Ten Categories of Being

Ontology proceeds to find out what it is that constitutes a being. What are the elements that make up a thing or a being? Ontology lists ten categories or classes applicable only to real (not logical), finite beings. It is also possible to group or list all ideas about beings under these categories. The ten categories are:

1. Substance
2. Quantity

3. Quality
4. Relation
5. Place
6. Time
7. Posture
8. Habit
9. Action
10. Passion

These ten categories[12] are really two categories—substance and accidents—since items 2 through 10 are accidents. *Substance*, *nature*, and *essence* are synonymous. They provide answers to the questions What is it? or Who is it? Substance refers to a being whose nature it is to exist in itself and not in something else. An accident, on the other hand, such as size, shape or color, is unable to exist in itself and exists only in a substance. Substance supports accidents.

The following little poem explains the ten categories of being. The corresponding number appears after the appropriate category.

> The tree (1) shades (9) the small (2) slaves (4)
>   Worn-out (10) by the summer's heat (3)
> Since noon (6) they lie (7) on the ground (5)
>   In garments (8) clean and neat.

Philosophers do not agree on the meaning of substance. Some, including John Locke, held that substance is something unknown and unknowable. According to Locke, substance is an unchanging kernel around which accidents are the rind. René Descartes held that substance is something earthless, and Immanuel Kant maintained that substance is something made up by human minds, or a "subjective form." Although these philosophers held different views on the nature of substance, all except Descartes admitted that accidents such as color, size and shape exist, or have a reality. Descartes denied that accidents have any reality. Scholastic philosophers, on the other hand, argue that it is possible for human beings to gain some knowledge of essence, although the knowledge gained may be imperfect.

Besides discussing the substance of things, ontology also deals with existence. In addition to determining what an object is, ontology asks *if* the object exists. It defines existence as the actual (as opposed to potential) presence of an object in the physical order. A great debate surrounds the distinction between essence and existence. Are these the same thing? An example may help to clarify the problem. When a sculptor makes a statue, does he or she produce two realities—the essence of the statue and its existence, or only one reality, the existing statue?

The Causes of Being

While ontology devotes considerable discussion to the ten categories of real being, it reserves the most important discussion for causality. Aristotle contributed significantly to the meaning and ramifications of causality. Ontology investigates what causes things or beings to exist (existence) and what makes them be what they are (essence). Thus, causality is of interest to students in most disciplines.

Ontology defines a *cause* as anything that positively influences in any way the being or essence of another thing. There cannot be a cause unless something other than the cause itself is produced, and that is an effect. The effects produced are either new beings or changes in existing things. Causes usually precede effects. While succession generally suggests causality, it is not sufficient to be a cause. Because one train follows another on a track does not mean that the first train is the cause of the second or third trains.

But this is exactly what some philosophers, such as John Locke, David Hume and John Stuart Mill, held. They claimed that people know only what their senses tell them. They argued that other philosophers have confused the notion of causality with succession. The senses (sight, hearing, touch, taste and smell) provide only the outward appearances of things or phenomena. These phenomena may or may not have a real existence. We cannot know anything about their essence or causes.

The realist school maintains there is a real world with real objects distinct from people. Changes do occur in these real objects. There are four types of causes involved to explain change or effects: (1) material causes, or the matter out of which something is made; (2) formal causes, or that by which an effect is constituted as a special kind of thing; (3) efficient causes, or those which make or bring about something; and (4) final causes (teleological), or the purpose(s) for which something is made. These four causes answer the following questions: From what was this object made? What makes it be this kind of object? Who made it? For what purpose? Developed by Aristotle, this school argues that there is a difference between cause and succession. Because night follows day does not mean that the day causes night. While human beings may experience an event such as a traffic accident only once, they can correctly distinguish between the cause(s) and effect(s) of such an event.

Discussion of material and formal causes is an important part of ontology. These notions deal with matter and form—matter being something indefinite and form being something very definite and specific that makes a particular body be what it is. This is the hylomorphic theory, which means that matter and form make up material things. St. Thomas Aquinas and his followers argued that both efficient and formal causes exist. They said that one thing acts as a cause and produces an effect by exercising a positive influence. They also argue that efficient causes act for a purpose (final causes).

Some empiricists deny the existence of both efficient and final causes. They maintain that all causality is unknown and unknowable, just as substance or essence is unknown and unknowable. People cannot know anything beyond what their senses tell them. They cannot deal with effects. They can deal only with material things. There are no spiritual beings—there is no spiritual soul. To help John Locke arrive at this philosophy, a group associated with Cambridge Platonism influenced him. Although Locke rejected their notion of the existence of innate ideas, he was sympathetic to their rejection of materialism or the existence of material objects. And while John Locke had significant influence on the formation of the U.S. system of government,[13] his rejection of the notions of cause and effect apparently has not influenced subsequent researchers and scientists.[14]

Yet the notions of cause and effect are at the root of all traditional research. Researchers assume that there is a real, physical world distinct from human beings; that change beginning with a *terminus a quo* (starting point), a transition and a *terminus ad quem* (finishing point) occurs in that physical world; that the causes of change can be determined; and that effects result from causes. Phenomenologists deny such notions as cause and effect and maintain that the closest we can come to explaining the world is by getting as close as possible to the objects portrayed by our senses and giving them meaning. This approach has wide application to organizational theory, organizational behavior and ethics. It is the foundation of the teleological approach to ethics.

Undoubtedly, ontology establishes the direction from which all sciences, including ethics, proceed. The arguments originating with Aristotle supporting the existence of a real world external to human beings and the existence of causality are so compelling that most sciences proceed on the assumption that such a real world exists.[15] However, the arguments of the Platonic school have attracted many scholars who subscribe to phenomenology and solipsism. Empiricists have also influenced some modern philosophers to think in terms of suspending reality and causality, and concentrate on the meaning of things as presented by the senses. When the issue of the certainty and validity of human knowledge is added to this debate, as the next chapter on epistemology does, there are more compelling reasons for the existence of two different approaches to the sciences and particularly to ethics.

NOTES

1. Gibson Burrell and Gareth Morgan, *Sociological Paradigms and Organizational Analysis* (Portsmouth, N.H.: Heinemann, 1985), p. x.

2. Antonio Rosmini, *The Origin of Ideas* (London: Tench and Company, 1883).

3. J.A.K. Thomson, ed., *The Ethics of Aristotle* (London: Penguin Books, 1955), pp. 350–51.

4. Ibid., pp. 35–56.

5. Anton C. Pegis, ed., *Basic Writings of Saint Thomas Aquinas*, Volume One (New York: Random House, 1945), pp. xxxv–liii.

6. Burrell and Morgan, *Sociological Paradigms*, pp. 31, 33, 278–79.

7. Ibid., p. viii.

8. Ibid., p. 239.

9. Anton C. Pegis, ed., *Basic Writings of Saint Thomas Aquinas*, Volume Two (New York: Random House, 1945), pp. 794–96.

10. Ibid., p. 799.

11. Michael J. Curtis, ed., *The Great Political Theories*, Volume 1 (New York: Avon Books, 1961), p. 325.

12. Thomson, *The Ethics of Aristotle*, p. 353.

13. John Locke, *Two Treatises on Government*, Peter Laslett, ed. (New York: Cambridge University Press, 1960).

14. John Locke, *Essay Concerning Human Understanding* (London: 1690).

15. Thomson, *The Ethics of Aristotle*, p. 353.

CHAPTER 3

Epistemology and Psychology as Roots of Ethics

EPISTEMOLOGY

Following a smattering of ontology, students may feel satisfied that a real, physical, external world exists. But this satisfaction is short lived. Some philosophers, while admitting that such a world exists, claim that even if it does, we can know little or nothing about it. They question the existence, reliability and validity of human knowledge. Here is where epistemology begins.

While ontology concentrates on the study of beings, the different kinds of beings and causality, epistemology focuses on whether human knowledge provides us with real insight into beings or whether it is merely a cobweb spun by the mind with no relationship to real things. Epistemology, therefore, examines the validity and certitude of human knowledge. Ontology focuses on the nature of beings or things; epistemology concentrates on how human beings know these things and on the faculties by which they acquire knowledge of beings or things.

Knowledge appears to be the simplest human experience. People seem to know and take for granted that things exist and that they have knowledge of these things. To most people all human knowledge can be summarized in the following sentence: The world I know is objectively real and I have a genuine knowledge of it as it is. This sentence summarizes ontology and epistemology. But it also raises difficulties. Apparently obvious and transparent explanations will not satisfy the human mind's quest for truth.

In the course of human development, many ordinary beliefs and convictions had to be discarded. For example, for thousands of years people believed that the earth was stationary at the center of the universe and that the sun, moon and stars revolved around it. The advancement of knowledge proved that this belief was erroneous. This is an example of the issues concerning the knowledge we have and with which epistemology deals.

Since epistemology focuses on human knowledge, there are four states or conditions of the human mind regarding knowledge: (1) ignorance or no knowledge in a subject capable of knowing something; (2) doubt or a state of mind in which the human subject is aware of an object but unable to assent to a judgment about it; (3) opinion or provisional assent to a judgment; and (4) certitude or assent given in a fixed and firm manner.

There are three kinds of certitude: (a) metaphysical, as when John McLaughlin, in TV's "The McLaughlin Group" uses a scale of 1 to 10, with a 10 as excluding all fear of error—could not be otherwise—as in the statement "A square is not a circle and could not be"; (2) physical, based on the consistency of the laws of nature and thus excluding prudent fear of error, as in my statement "I am certain the sun will rise tomorrow"; and (3) moral, or based on the way people commonly act, as in the statement, "Parents love their children." While some deny that physical and moral certitude belong in the same classification with metaphysical certitude, and constitute little more than an opinion, philosophers generally agree that they are lesser forms of certitude.

Later discussion in this chapter will show that all knowledge arises from judgments. There are five kinds of judgment: (1) judgments arising from sense experience, as in "Today is cold"; (2) immediate, self-evident necessary judgments arrived at by analyzing and comparing abstract ideas, such as $2 + 2 = 4$ or "The whole is greater than the part"; (3) mediate necessary judgments, or judgments derived from truths already known but are not in themselves *immediately* evident; (4) judgments arrived at by generalizations—that is, generalizing by inductive reasoning from particular cases to universals by the principle of causality and the universality of the laws of nature; although contrary to the principles of logic, the laws of physics—such as illumination or gravity—are derived in this manner; (5) judgments on the authority of another person, depending on the credence we give the other person, the credentials a person has, his or her veracity, and so on.

Over the centuries, many skeptics have doubted the power of the human mind to know the truth. They have pointed out that frequently people have been in error unknown to themselves, as when they see a straight stick appear crooked when placed in a glass of water. The error of observation seems in no way different from the truth. Others claim that epistemology can and must analyze all judgments through a methodology called *methodic doubt*. This is not *real* doubt, but a method a person can voluntarily use to question or analyze a judgment about which the intellect is certain that the judgment under examination is true. It is similar to playing devil's advocate.

René Descartes used this approrach to an extreme. Descartes claimed that the only way to find objective truth is by attempting to doubt absolutely every judgment. If any judgment resists a person's best efforts to doubt it, that judgment is an absolute certainty. Then by using this truth as a foundation, it is possible to build up some other truths that are also absolutely certain. According to Descartes, he succeeded in doubting every judgment except one—the fact of his own existence. He expressed this finding as follows: "*Cogito. Ergo sum*" ("I think. Therefore, I exist").

Many critics deny that Descartes succeeded in doubting his own existence, or that he could doubt immediate, self-evident judgments in the first place. In fact, some claim that he used implicitly the principle of contradiction throughout his doubting process. Others say if Descartes did indeed succeed in doubting all immediate, self-evident necessary judgments, he should have succeeded in doubting the judgment "I exist."

In spite of the problems inherent in this approach to epistemology, the objectives are quite clear: Are the objects people know real things; or, even if knowledge is objective, can people know real things with certitude? As the previous chapter pointed out, there are two main opposing schools of thought: realism and idealism.

Realism as taught by many philosophers, including Aristotle, maintains that a real, physical world exists distinct from ourselves. It further stipulates that human beings can and do know objects distinct from themselves and their own minds, and that they can know these things with certainty. The Platonic school, on the other hand, and the idealists do not accept the existence of an objective world. Idealism claims that only an ideal world exists and denies the existence of real things. Even if there were an objective world, the idealist or Platonist denies that people can have valid and reliable knowledge of it.

Epistemology, therefore, examines the human cognitive faculties to decide if these faculties can provide genuine, objective knowledge—or knowledge merely created by these faculties. According to Aristotle and St. Thomas Aquinas, there are two cognitive faculties by which people acquire knowledge: (1) the five senses and (2) the intellect.[1]

The Validity of Sense Knowledge

By the senses, people acquire knowledge of concrete, material things, including their own bodies. A major problem here is the trustworthiness of the senses. For thousands of years people believed what their senses taught them—that the earth was at the center of the universe and that the sun, moon and stars revolved around it. Since this theory is not correct, it calls into question the trustworthiness of the human senses at least in certain cases. In examining the objectivity of sense knowledge, philosophers have proposed idealism and realism.

Idealism states that the objects of both sense and intellectual knowledge are mental, not real. People cannot know real things through their senses—they can know only impressions or states. Some idealists such as Bishop Berkeley admit that the human mind, the minds of others and the mind of God are indeed real, but nothing else may be real. Other idealists such as Immanuel Kant claim that there may be a real world out there, but human beings have no knowledge of it.

Besides past sense errors, the main argument supporting idealism is that knowledge by its very nature is mental. It is an action that occurs within people, and the product of that action must itself be mental. It has no effect on or relationship with things external to people, if indeed such things exist. Berkeley states that some things such as a toothache exist only when they are perceived. These objects depend on a person's perception for their existence. It is foolish, he says, to state that things exist unperceived. This argument is the idealist postulate, or the principle of immanence. This principle means that knowledge remains within a person and cannot reach out. The only knowable reality things have is their perceived reality—that is, things can be known only insofar as a person can perceive them. Perceived reality exists in the perceiver, just as the reality of a toothache exists only in its perceiver (sufferer). The expression *esse est percipi* (to exist means to be perceived) sums up this theory. All things people know have no reality other than what they have because of being perceived by human minds. Knowledge of its very nature is the state of the knowing mind. The known object, therefore, must be something in the mind—something the mind creates. Descartes and Kant contended that the mind cannot have knowledge of matter, but only of spiritual or mental ideas. If an external world exists, it is the artefact of the human mind and consciousness has created it.

The idealist postulate arises from the difficulty of understanding how the mind can transcend itself and contact other things—how does the mind become aware of itself or indeed of anything else? In fact, the idealist postulate confuses two different propositions, one of which is self-evident and the other which is an unproved assumption. The self-evident principle is that which is known by the mind must be brought into relation to the mind. For example, I know nothing about trees in the Black Forest or of a person whom I have never seen or heard. This is self-evident. There cannot be a *perceived object except while it is being perceived*. This is quite different from stating that there *cannot be an object except while it is being perceived*. In the first case, the idealist is stating that I cannot *perceive* a tree in the Black Forest except while *actually perceiving* it. That is not the same as stating that the tree in the Black Forest does not exist until I perceive it. The latter is not self-evident, whereas the former is.

Idealists address the issue of sense illusions. The example given of the stick in the glass of water illustrates this point. If a person observes a stick in an open area, it appears straight. If he or she places the same stick in a glass of water, it appears crooked. The same stick cannot be crooked and straight simultaneously. The idealist concludes that the observer does not see the stick at all, or that it does not exist. This argument, of course, is contradictory. Since the idealist does not recognize the existence of the stick in the first place, the conclusions in both situations should have been the same: the observer does not see the stick at all, the straight stick does not exist, the crooked stick does not exist.

Realism states that real, external, extramental objects exist and that we can know at least some of them. One branch of realism—representationalism—states that the direct object of human knowledge is a mental object, but by inference people can acquire a second-hand knowledge of the corresponding, external real object. This theory is a slight expansion of the idealist postulate and is subject to the same shortcomings. A second brand of realism—perceptionalism—claims that, at least sometimes, the direct object of knowledge is external, extramental reality. Perceptionalists differ on the extent to which people know extramental reality.

The theories of idealism and realism arise from difficulties involved with human sense perception. Philosophers from Aristotle onward have divided sense qualities into proper and common sensibles, or as modern scholars call them, primary and secondary qualities. A *common sensible* is one that can be perceived by more than one of our senses, such as extension or movement. A *proper sensible* can be perceived by only one sense, such as color, sound, smell, cold or heat. Modern philosophers imply that the primary sensibles are more real or objective than the secondary sensibles, which are more subjective.

To be aware of anything, it is not sufficient that a human mind exists and that a quality exists. There also must be a sense organ. People become aware of an object only through the action of the sense organ. For example, a person without sight does not become aware of color. Objects presented by the sense organs owe their quality partly to the object itself, partly to the medium between the sense organ and the object and partly to the condition of the sense organ itself. When the senses appear to err, as in assessing the stick in a glass of water, the error is one of *judgment* by which the observer doesn't consider the condition or medium when observing the same stick out of water. It is not the sense organ but the intellect that corrects that illusion, or any illusion of that kind.

Immanuel Kant was aware of the problems involved with sense perception. Kant was a partial idealist to the extent that, for him, the only objects people can know are mental states or ideas. Other things may exist, but people cannot know them. According to Kant, there are in the human sense faculties two "gates" through which everything must pass—namely, space and time. Human beings can know objects only after they enter the mind through these two gates. The objects people know appear to exist in space and time. In the intellect, he says, there are twelve similar passages or entry points corresponding to the ten categories of being. These twelve categories are *a priori* forms. Every idea of which a person is aware must have passed through one of these twelve *a priori* forms. Therefore, every idea appears as a substance or an accident according to the *a priori* form through which it entered.

While Kant provided several arguments for the existence of both types of sense data entry points, it is unclear that he adequately established time and space as qualities of the senses and not of things existing in space and time.

The Validity or Objectivity of Intellectual Knowledge

The foregoing discussion focused on one cognitive faculty—the senses—by which people acquire knowledge. There is a second cognitive faculty, the intellect. The intellect enables people to acquire concepts and form judgments from which they reason to other judgments. The science of logic examines this process, but epistemology focuses on the *value* of the knowledge acquired from this process. It concentrates on the objectivity of concepts, of judgments and of reasoning. The processes of reasoning and of judgment are particularly applicable to ethics, especially in discussing conscience, which from an interpretivist or objectivist perspective involves making a practical judgment of the goodness or badness of a human action.[2]

The Objectivity of Concepts

Does the formation of concepts provide us with any knowledge of reality, or is it only the senses that provide objective knowledge? This question focuses on the difference between *perceived objects* and *conceived objects*, or between percepts and concepts. The senses provide us with percepts. Besides percepts, upon reflection or the process of introspection, we become aware of other ideas or concepts, or *conceived objects*, in our minds, such as man, animal, truth, goodness, beauty and an array of abstract ideas. The issue here is the value or validity of these abstract ideas.

We derive all our knowledge from judgments. If we never form a judgment, as far as the advancement of knowledge is concerned, we are no better than animals. Our senses provide us with only the raw materials—the data—for forming judgments. But every judgment contains as one of its elements at least one abstract concept. Some judgments contain two or more abstract concepts, in both subject and predicate, as in the statement: 2 (abstract) + 2 (abstract) = 4 (abstract). Other judgments involve a *concept* and a *percept*. We are constantly identifying the two, as in the example, "John (percept) is a man (concept)." Some philosophers claim that unless concepts are objective realities, all such judgments are useless and meaningless. If all our abstract ideas are solely mental objects, all our knowledge is subjective. This is the problem of universals because conceived objects are universal concepts. Every perceived object is one, singular, concrete and incommunicable entity, while every conceived object is one or many, universal and abstract. The problem arises from the identification of the one with the other, especially because of the total dissimilarity between concepts and percepts. And yet we continue to identify one with the other. In an attempt to resolve this problem, we encounter the two philosophical schools of realism and idealism.

Extreme realists maintain that concepts are real things; they really exist somewhere. When our intellects form universal concepts, these forms are present to our intellects, just as our senses form percepts when sense objects are present to our senses. Plato claimed that concepts existed in the world of suprasensible ideas, which transcends and is separate from the sense world. In addressing our tendency to identify concepts with percepts, Plato spoke of sense objects (percepts) as sharing or participating in the reality of universals (concepts), similar to a shadow's having some relation to the reality that cast the shadow.

Moderate realism as propounded by St. Thomas Aquinas holds that the objects of our universal concepts are real objects, but the qualities we conceive these objects have do not belong to them in reality. Objects such as "man" or "virtue" really exist, but their universality and abstract character do not exist. Our intellects clothe real objects in abstract qualities. There is no contradiction in stating that conceived objects are contained in perceived objects and are identical to them. The two are the same object made present to us by two different faculties, the senses and the intellect. The concept "man," in the sentence "John is a man," appears to have properties entirely opposite the percept "John," only because the intellect has added these additional properties to it. St. Thomas Aquinas sums up the distinction between percepts and concepts, or between the senses and the intellect, as follows: *"Nihil est in intellectu quod non prius fuerit in sensu"* ("There is nothing in the intellect that did not previously exist in the senses").[3]

Any object to become present to us must accommodate itself to the nature of the faculty that presents it. The intellect as established in psychology is a spiritual faculty. To be present to the intellect, any material object must be dematerialized or spiritualized—that is, it becomes present to it in an abstract form. In reality, when we say "John is a man," we are stating that, in fact, there is only one, single object—John. We acquire knowledge of that object by two different faculties, the senses and the intellect. As a result, it appears that we are aware of two objects instead of one. Our concepts are dependent on our percepts or on the raw data provided by the senses through percepts. This is particularly obvious in the example of a person deprived of hearing from birth, a result of which he or she is unable to form a concept of sound. St. Thomas Aquinas summarizes moderate realism in this way: *"Cognitum est in cognoscente secundum modum cognoscentis"* ("A known object is in the knowing mind according to the manner of the knower").[4]

The theory of conceptualism claims that conceived objects are not real. Our intellectual activity creates these objects, and they are at the most logical beings that have no reality at all. Nominalism is another version of conceptualism. This theory states that conceived objects are neither real nor logical beings; they are nothing but mere words or names. There are no universal concepts in reality, or even in our minds. There are only universal words or names such as *man, animal, virtue*. These universal names happen to correspond with what the realists call objective reality. The major proponents of this theory are Bishop Berkeley and John Stuart Mill and, to a certain extent, John Locke.

The root of nominalism is that the human mind lacks a power or faculty higher than the senses, and therefore cannot and does not perceive an object that is universal. Since the senses can apprehend only objects that are individual and concrete, it is impossible to perceive an object that is genuinely universal. Nominalists deny that universal objects exist even as objects of thought.[5]

Why do we apply a common name to several individuals (such as *man* to represent all men and women) when nominalists claim that no universals exist? Nominalists explain that corresponding to the common name *man*, there exists a mental image made up of several individual images that are vague, blurred and indistinct, and that we mistake that mental image for a universal concept. Nominalists admit that words such as *man* are universal while the blurred image obtains whatever universality it may have from its association with the word itself. This appears to be putting the cart before the horse inasmuch as it claims that images are derived from words (thoughts) rather than words derived from thoughts or images.

Another version of nominalism is positivism. This theory claims that material reality reveals itself to the senses, and this is the sole object of our knowledge. Metaphysical and immaterial objects—such as beings, substance, spirits—are only an illusion. Similar to nominalism, it claims that there is in humans no faculty higher than the senses and we know nothing beyond the material world. This leads to denying the existence of a spiritual world, which theodicy and psychology address. Advocates of this theory provided the basis for Marxism and, ultimately, communism.

The objectivity of concepts is a major issue in epistemology. The previous discussion has focused on some key factors involving concepts and precepts, and essentially provided two alternative main theories with moderate realism serving as an intermediate between them. But since concepts by themselves do not provide knowledge, it is necessary to examine judgments that do.

The Objectivity of Judgments

To have knowledge, we form or make judgments—that is, we decide mentally whether one concept agrees or disagrees with another. What is it that causes us to affirm or deny one concept over another? The first major issue here is the validity of *immediate, self-evident, necessary judgments or first principles*. For example, when we say that $2 + 2 = 4$, we note that our minds have set up a relationship between the subject and predicate that is absolutely necessary (could not be otherwise) and universal (true in every instance—metaphysical certitude). Is it the nature of the subject and predicate that causes us to reach that conclusion, or is it our experience with that sort of subject and that sort of predicate? Some philosophers say it is our experience that causes us to reach the conclusion and here our judgment is objective. Others claim that the only explanation for reaching this kind of judgment is in the mind itself and is, therefore, subjective.

Immanuel Kant and John Stuart Mill argued that necessary judgments are subjective. Kant, as discussed previously in this chapter, explains that the necessary connection between subject and predicate as arising from the existence in our intellects of twelve *a priori* gates, through which all knowledge must pass before emerging into the conscious mind. In passing through a particular *a priori* gate, the noumenon (which is unknowable in itself before entering the *a priori* gate) is stamped or marked by the particular *a priori* gate and thus this stamp turns the noumenon into a phenomenon, or something known to the mind only after passing through a particular *a priori* gate. Experience tells us that in particular instances $2 + 2 = 4$. We find this judgment in our minds with necessity and universality. The *a priori* gate through which this knowledge entered our consciousness stamped on it the qualities of necessity and universality.

This is a subjective theory that explains judgments by something in the human mind. To arrive at this theory, Kant divided all judgments into analytic and synthetic. Kant describes analytic judgments as those where the predicate can be found in the subject through analyzing the subject. Definitions are analytic judgments as, for example, the human is a rational animal. Kant claimed that these kinds of judgments are small in number and unimportant. Synthetic judgments, on the other hand, are those where the truth is obtained not from analyzing the subject but *from experience*. Some of these are synthetic *a posteriori* judgments that are based solely on experience—as, for example, the statement, "I am writing." Synthetic *a priori* judgments, on the other hand, contain something more than what experience alone provides. Something in the unconscious mind besides experience enables us to make the judgment $2 + 2 = 4$. To establish this point, Kant examined what he called four synthetic judgments, such as mathematical judgments. It appears that mathematical judgments, such as $2 + 2 = 4$, are analytic judgments, arrived at by *analyzing* and comparing the subject and the predicate.

John Stuart Mill said that we establish a relationship between subject and predicate, not because we see such a relationship to exist, but because the subject and predicate have been associated regularly with each other and our minds are so constructed by the laws of association that we cannot recall one concept without the other. This is a completely subjective theory based on the laws of association.

Scholastic philosophers maintain that the human intellect establishes universal and necessary connections between subjects and predicates, not because its own nature compels it to do so, as Kant and Mill maintained, but because the subject and predicate *demand* such a connection. The connection is as much an objective fact as the subject and predicate themselves. The human mind does not make the connection; it *discovers* that the connection already exists. The connection becomes objectively evident to the intellect.

In trying to establish the objectivity of the connection, scholastic philosophers argue that while the senses make us aware of things as they appear to be, even when such appearances are not correct—as exemplified by a stick appearing crooked in a glass of water—it is not the senses that correct the illusion but rather the intellect. The stick in a glass of water will still appear crooked to the senses, but the intellect is not compelled to assent to things as they appear. Mere awareness of things is not knowledge attained by an intellectual act of judgment. Introspection allows the intellect to refrain from immediate judgments until it has an opportunity to analyze or compare subject with predicate. When the relationship becomes perfectly clear, the intellect must assent to the relationship and make the judgment. In this instance, the judgment of the intellect is objective and self-evident.

In addition to self-evident, necessary judgments or first principles, there are also judgments that are not self-evident or *mediate necessary judgments*. These judgments are derived by deductive reasoning from self-evident necessary judgments. This involves the validity of syllogistic reasoning. Is deductive reasoning a valid process? Does it lead to knowledge, and, if so, to knowledge of reality? This is particularly applicable to the study of ethics from either a deontological or a teleological perspective. If our knowledge is or can be invalid, surely our ethical judgments arrived at by deductive reasoning may also be invalid.

Some philosophers claim that every syllogism is invalid, that every syllogism involves "begging the question" (*petitio principii*). For example, they claim that the syllogism, "All men are mortal. John is a man. Therefore John is mortal," involves the fallacy of begging the question. The conclusion to be proved that John is mortal is already taken as true in the major premise "All men are mortal." John Stuart Mill claimed that we cannot know the major premise to be true unless we know the conclusion to be true. We must know that every person is mortal before we can subscribe to the validity of the major premise.

Other philosophers deny that syllogistic reasoning involves begging the question. They claim that syllogistic reasoning, in stating a major premise, involves analysis of the concepts contained in it. Thus the major premise "All men are mortal" involves analysis of two abstract concepts, "man" and "mortal." We do not consider individual men in this analysis, as Mill claims.

So the process does not involve begging the question—that is, we do not know the conclusion when we analyze the concepts in the major premise.

The debate between the two schools involves the paradox of inference. If deductive reasoning is worth anything, it must allow us to advance from premises already known to a conclusion previously unknown, as the syllogism just discussed shows. On the other hand, if deductive reasoning is to be valid, the premises must already contain the conclusion—otherwise, the conclusion cannot be drawn from them. The paradox is that while the conclusion is new, the premise still contains the conclusion.

The resolution of this paradox, whether real or apparent, involves a distinction between actual knowledge and potential knowledge, or between the explicit and implicit. Philosophers argue that, to be valid, the conclusion does not need to be *explicitly* contained in the premises, only *implicitly*. Thus, the conclusion drawn by syllogistic reasoning advances knowledge in that it makes explicit that which was only implicitly contained in the premise. Finally, while logic prohibits us from arguing from the particular to the general, two laws—the principle of causality discussed in chapter 2, and the principle of the uniformity of nature—often enable researchers to arrive at accurate conclusions through inductive reasoning. However, it is clear that such methodologies require rigorous, prolonged testing to eliminate the errors to which inductive reasoning is subject. All laws of physics are so discovered.

While epistemology is the philosophical science concerned with the validity and certitude of human knowledge, it has important ramifications for ethics. If our human knowledge is not valid and reliable, then the ethical judgments and decisions we make may also be invalid and erroneous. Consequently, epistemology is the foundation upon which the validity and certitude of ethical decisions are built. It also provides the basis for two schools of thought in ethics. But before entering the science of ethics, it is important in this smattering of philosophy to review briefly the psychological constitution of humans in the science of psychology.

SCHOLASTIC PSYCHOLOGY

Psychology began with Aristotle, who wrote a treatise entitled "On the Soul." But subsequent scholars neglected psychology until St. Thomas Aquinas revived it in the thirteenth century. It is now known as scholastic psychology. Scholastic psychology concentrates on the study of human beings, including the body, bodily organs, senses, nerves, memory, imagination, the will and the soul. It is not the same as modern psychology.

The latter is concerned with the behavior of human beings. To a large extent, it does not focus on normal, average human beings and the powers they possess. It concentrates on the human mind, the human soul. But in doing so, it investigates phenomena such as human sensations, perceptions, thoughts, volitions and emotions. We call this part of psychology empirical psychology because we experience the phenomena studied. Rational psychology examines the source or principle behind these activities. It derives information about the nature of the mind or the soul, not through experience, but through reasoning.

The methodology of psychology is largely that of introspection—that is, an examination of the human mind by the human mind itself. The observer and the observed are the same. This approach is somewhat flawed, but is helped by contributions of scholars who have studied their own human minds and their operations, and recorded the results of these studies.

Psychology and epistemology are interdependent. Psychology overlaps epistemology to the extent that it deals to some extent with the same subject matter—the intellect and the senses. But epistemology is limited to the study of these two cognitive faculties to decide if use of these faculties leads to valid knowledge. Psychology is broader in that it examines *all* mental faculties, including impulses, habits, emotions, feelings, memory, imagination, appetites, instincts and character. Psychology studies these faculties to *describe how they work.* It assumes from epistemology that human beings can acquire a genuine knowledge of their own minds and their operations. Thus epistemology is the forerunner of psychology. Epistemology depends on psychology for data supporting the existence and functioning of the human senses and the intellect.

Psychology is the foundation of ethics. It examines the *causes* of human actions, whereas the main concerns of ethics are the *consequences* (the goodness or badness) of these same actions. Psychology also studies such issues as free will, conscience and habits, which are the cornerstone of ethics.

Empirical psychology first focuses on the notion of sensation, which (according to moderate realism) is the reaction of the human mind to an external object. This involves a description of the external object, the sense or senses to which it is exposed and the impression made on the brain. Thus, psychology describes how the five human senses operate and the pathologies that affect them. It also describes the human nervous system, the brain and its parts, memory and imagination. It explains how sensations and illusions occur. Physiology, which studies how our physical organs work, provides us with some of the same information as empirical psychology, except that empirical psychology sees activities of the senses as working through bodily organs.

Rational psychology attempts to anlayze *how* concepts are formed. One group of scholastic psychologists claims that human knowledge first comes through the senses. But the process of forming concepts involves four stages: (1) the impression is produced by the sense faculty or the percept; (2) a concrete image is formed on the imagination—the phantasm; (3) the spiritual power or the *intellectus agens* moves the mind to act; (4) the intellect produces a concept.

The two major issues in rational psychology are free will and the human soul. These two topics are especially germane to the study of ethics.

Free Will

No topic is more applicable to ethics than free will. If human beings do not have free will, they are not responsible for their actions. There is no point in discussing human actions or their morality if another source determines these actions and human beings have no control over them. So free will is a major issue in both psychology and ethics. St. Thomas Aquinas addressed free will at length as well as the relationship of the will to the intellect.[6]

The will is a human faculty that enables a person to strive after something apprehended as good. *Free will* means that the will has the power to act *or* not to act in a particular manner when all the conditions for acting are present. Free will pertains to moral liberty as opposed to physical liberty, or immunity from restraint in external actions, and as opposed to civil liberty, which is immunity from state compulsion in the exercise of a right not contrary to the common good. Civil liberty, for example, does not exist in prison but moral liberty can.

Free will does not mean that all human actions are free. Human beings perform many actions that are not free, such as the beating of our heart and other automatic actions. Other actions are not free because we give no thought to them. Free will means that at least some human actions are free, yet character, circumstances and motivation can and may influence us. And while it is possible to predict accurately in certain circumstances how an individual will act, it is also clear that circumstances may influence a person's actions but do not determine them.

The theory of *determinism*, on the other hand, holds that the human will is not free and that circumstances and antecedents inevitably guide all human actions. Human beings are products of the environment that sets the course of human action.

Psychologists offer several arguments to validate the notion of free will. One is that people must do good, but they do not always do it. There can be no obligation to do the impossible (which determinism suggests). Therefore, a person could have done the good action when he actually did not. This shows that at least some human actions are free.

A second argument favoring free will is that consciousness tells us we have the power to choose and select our actions. When we reflect on ourselves, we are aware that we are the cause of our thoughts. We guide the course of our thoughts, selecting one train of thought while rejecting another. Reflection tells us that the more forcible train does not compel us to select it. This thought process shows that at least in our thoughts we have free will.

The process of deliberation involves a similar conclusion. When a person is confronted with two or more possible courses of action, she deliberates, considers the merits of each course, and perhaps even decides to wait before deciding. The act of choosing among two or more alternatives provides strong evidence that the will is not determined but, rather, is free.

The Human Soul

Besides investigating and describing the mental activities of human beings and establishing that human beings have free will, rational psychology also investigates the principle or cause of psychic and mental activities. In pursuing this course of action, psychology borrows from logic and epistemology. It uses both inductive and deductive reasoning to arrive at the cause of human mental activity. Through inductive reasoning, psychology begins with particular truths and argues to the general cause from which they spring. The argument is that the operations of an object signify what the nature of the object is (*Qualis est operatio, talis est natura*).[7] Following the inductive reasoning, psychology uses deductive reasoning to reach other conclusions about the origin and destiny of the soul.

Psychologists initially use the word *soul* to mean the *ultimate* source, the principle or cause of all mental activity. From epistemology it is clear that concepts, thoughts and abstract ideas are not material things; they have become *dematerialized* on the way from the senses to the intellect. Therefore, their root cause cannot be anything material. The senses or brain are not sufficient cause to explain these effects. So relying on human reason alone, psychology attempts to find the ultimate explanation for these mental activities—it states that the soul is the ultimate cause of mental activities. St. Thomas Aquinas, while providing elaborate thought on all aspects of the soul, defines the soul as "the first principle of life in those things in our world which live."[8]

The first premise of psychologists is that the soul is a *substance* that ontology defines as that which exists in itself and does not depend on anything else for its existence. Philosophers such as John Locke, Immanuel Kant and the phenomenologists, who deny the existence of substance or who say it is unknown and unknowable, deny that the human soul is a substance.

Psychology offers several arguments to show that the soul is a substance. Everyone admits that mental acts are actions and modifications. Actions and modifications imply a substantial principle in which they exist and from which they proceed. For example, there cannot be pain without a subject to feel it. Thoughts and acts of the will presuppose something that thinks and wills. The Principle of Sufficient Reason enters here by claiming that it is illogical to proceed indefinitely to find a sufficient reason for something. We must ultimately arrive at something that exists in itself—in the case of the soul, a substantial principle is the source of all mental activity.

Another argument is as follows. We are unable to explain or understand our mental activities without a substantial principle from which they proceed. For example, our faculty of reproducing past sensations and recognizing them now as past is inexplicable unless those past sensations produced some impression on us and we now reproduce the past impression. Since the past impression and current recognition are mental activities, the Principle of Sufficient Reason dictates that a material object such as the human brain is insufficient to explain these mental activities. This logically leads to the conclusion that the soul is a substance.

The soul is not only a substance, it is a *simple* substance—that is, it is not composite or made up of parts, as the human body or any material object is. In philosophical language, matter and form do not make up the soul as they do material objects. Therefore, it lacks constituent or external parts and it occupies no space.[9]

The argument supporting the simplicity of the soul arises because the soul performs actions or activities that composite beings (beings made up of parts) could not perform, such as the formation of abstract ideas, judgments, reasoning and acts of volition. By focusing on the formation of abstract ideas, such as unity, truth, goodness or virtue, we can see that these ideas are essentially simple. So the ultimate cause—the soul—of these ideas must itself be simple.

The process of judgment and reasoning provides further evidence that the soul is a simple substance. For example, consideration of the judgment "Man is mortal" leads to the conclusion that a composite substance could not make such a judgment. If the thinking substance—the soul—had parts, the following scenario would occur: Let x, y and z represent the parts of the above judgment. Let x represent the subject, man; y the predicate, mortal; and z, the verb, is. No judgment could result in this scenario because part x would retain the subject, part y the predicate and part z the verb, so that no comparison could be made between the three items. The most that could be said of this scenario is that all three parts could form separate judgments. But it is impossible to form three judgments since there is only one judgment involved. So it is reasonable to conclude that the soul must be a simple substance.

Psychology proceeds beyond the simplicity of the soul to establish that the soul is also spiritual.[10] Up to this point philosophers have claimed that all souls, including the souls of animals, are simple substances. What, if anything, differentiates human souls from the souls of animals? Psychologists answer that spirituality constitutes the essential difference.

Spirituality is not identical with simplicity, which, as stated above, means that a being does not have matter and form or parts. Although a spiritual substance is simple, spirituality goes beyond simplicity to include independence of matter—that is, a spiritual substance does not depend on any material object for its functioning; it can also perform at least some actions without any help from a material object. While a spiritual substance may perform certain activities *through* a material substance, as the human soul does through the brain and senses, in itself, it is independent of matter.

The argument supporting the spirituality of the soul is that the subject of spiritual activities must itself be spiritual. The soul is the subject of spiritual activities. Therefore the soul is spiritual.

"The subject of spiritual activities must itself be spiritual." This statement is just an application of the principle that the activities of a substance suggest the nature of a substance. It would be impossible for a material substance to perform spiritual activities or activities beyond the power of matter.[11]

The soul is the subject of spiritual activities. As already discussed and in epistemology, the human intellect performs activities such as the formation of abstract ideas, judgments and reasoning, which could not result from a material organ. Sense knowledge resulting from physical organs is always concrete and individual, whereas abstract ideas and judgments are not concrete and individual, but are stripped of individuality and concreteness—they are universal. The soul is the cause of these immaterial or spiritual activities. Therefore, the human soul must be spiritual.

Some philosophers deny the spirituality of the human soul, either maintaining that it is material since only matter exists or that through evolution, elements of "mind stuff" have evolved to endow some animals with more consciousness. The brain is the organ responsible for all animal activities. These theorists, however, do not offer cogent explanations of how a material substance can produce a spiritual activity, as discussed above.

But psychology is not content with providing strong evidence that the human soul is a simple, spiritual substance. It goes on to argue that the soul is also immortal. While there are several arguments to support this claim, the most cogent is a teleological argument.

All science proceeds from the assumption that the universe is rational—that reason and laws govern it. Everything has a purpose, including our bodies and our senses. Our senses of smell and taste exist because there are objects that satisfy them. The same is true of instincts—there must be objects to satisfy them. But the human mind has the power to look back into the indefinite past and forward to the distant future. There is an impulse of the mind to go beyond time and space and to conceive endless duration. It is reasonable to conclude that these characteristics of the human mind must have a corresponding object to satisfy them. The human mind's desire for a never-ending future cannot be left unsatisfied. The purpose of the human mind or soul provides a strong argument that the human soul must be immortal.[12]

Psychology also discusses the union of the human soul with the body, and the location of the soul within the body. Although it provides arguments to show that the soul works through bodily organs, it does not depend on them and death separates it from these organs. It also provides arguments to show that the soul is not located in any particular part of the body, but is a simple, spiritual substance in every part of the body. But human reason alone is limited in further exploring this point. When linked with theology, a clearer picture emerges.[13]

SUMMATION

The discussions of ontology, epistemology and psychology show the dependence of ethics on these sciences. At the same time, the theories presented indicate the limitations of human reason alone in establishing, with metaphysical certitude, answers to all basic questions. The same can be said about ethics—it will not provide answers to all questions nor answers with metaphysical certitude to some. Various theorists have also provided a basis for different thought in ethics and the following chapters elaborate on these theories by focusing on ethics.

NOTES

1. Anton C. Pegis, ed., *Basic Writings of Saint Thomas Aquinas*, Volume One (New York: Random House, 1945), pp. 805–30.

2. Ibid., pp. 793–827.

3. Ibid., p. 820.

4. Ibid., p. 817.

5. George H. Sabine and Thomas L. Thorson, *A History of Political Theory*, 4th edition (Hinsdale, Ill.: Dryden Press, 1973).

6. Pegis, *Basic Writings of Saint Thomas Aquinas*, pp. 777–92.

7. Anton C. Pegis, ed., *Basic Writings of Saint Thomas Aquinas*, Volume Two (New York: Random House, 1945), pp. 5–6.

8. Pegis, Vol. One, p. 683.

9. Ibid., p. 868.

10. Ibid., p. 683.

11. Ibid., pp. 682–744.

12. Ibid., pp. 691–92.

13. Ibid., pp. 695–718.

EDUARDO U. RODRIGUEZ GALVEZ
Relacionador Industrial

CHAPTER 4

The Focus of Ethics Is Human Action

DEFINITIONS OF ETHICS

Scholars often call ethics "moral philosophy."[1] The previous chapter showed that ethics is a branch of classical philosophy dealing with morality. It is closely related to and depends on other branches of philosophy. As noted in the previous chapter, theories relating to the existence of an external and real physical world, and to the capacity of the human mind to acquire knowledge, affect ethics. It should not be surprising, then, to discover that there is no single definition of *ethics*. There are different definitions arising from the various theories discussed. These definitions have their roots in the two basic philosophies of realism and idealism, or objectivism and interpretivism.

The objectivist-based definitions are all similar; they are deontological definitions. The following are two objectivist definitions of ethics:

The normative standards of conduct derived from the philosophical and religious traditions of society.[2]

The attempt to state and evaluate principles by which ethical problems may be solved.[3]

The classical scholastic definition of ethics is similar. Scholastic philosophers see ethics as the philosophical science that directs or guides voluntary human actions according to ultimate principles discovered by human reason alone. According to this definition, ethics is the science that relies on human reason to discover standards of conduct or morality that apply to all human beings. The previous chapter said that human reason alone has limits, and therefore it should not be surprising that these standards of morality also will have limitations.

The essential ingredient of the deontological definitions is that real, objective standards of morality exist for humans and that at least some of these standards can be discovered by human reason. Ethicists devote their energies to discovering such standards of conduct or codes of moral behavior. Organizations that have developed codes of ethics for their members, such as the American Medical Association and the American Society for Public Administration, subscribe to a deontological definition of ethics.

The interpretivist approach has a different definition of ethics. As discussed in the previous chapter, the interpretivist is an idealist who does not subscribe to the existence of a real, external world; even if he did, he would deny that human beings can have objective knowledge of it. For the interpretivist, a real world may or may not exist, and real, objective standards, laws or rules may or may not exist. So definitions from an interpretivist perspective are strictly teleological. The following are examples of interpretivist definitions of ethics:

Ethics introduces a radical kind of doubt into the everyday world. . . . Ethics looks at the future; it is concerned with the goodness and rightness of man's doing and making . . . it looks at the past for the sake of the future. . . . Ethics seeks to clarify the logic and the adequacy of the values that shape the world; it assesses the moral possibilities which are projected and portrayed in the social give-and-take. . . . Ethics is concerned with the intent morality in itself—with the moral quality of its orientation to the future and to relativism.[4]

The tasks of careful reflection several steps removed from the actual conduct of men concerning the assumptions and presumptions of the moral life.[5]

Cynthia McSwain and Orion White explain the teleological approach as follows: "Actors create meaning reflexively, through looking backward at their actions and interpreting them so as to build and maintain shared categories of common sense assumptions about 'what is going on,' and what is the correct way to behave."[6] McSwain and White admit that the interpretivist definitions of ethics seem to imply ethical relativism. But as chapters 2 and 3 pointed out, this definition has strong roots in both ontology and epistemology.

Those who subscribe to the teleological definitions of ethics are not trying to discover or develop standards of morality for people. They are attempting to interpret what meaning can be found in human actions and, through reflection, how right or wrong are these actions. Interpretivists may arrive at the same conclusion concerning the rightness or wrongness of a human action, but they do not derive their conclusions from objective rules, laws or standards.

Besides the above definitions is Jeremy Bentham's utilitarian definition: "Ethics at large may be defined as the art of directing men's actions to the greatest production of the greatest possible quantity of happiness on the part of those whose interest is in view. . . . Ethics . . . may be styled as the art of self-government."[7] I address this definition later in this chapter.

Jonsen and Hellegers describe ethics as "a body of prescriptions and prohibitions, do's and dont's, that people consider to carry uncommon weight in their lives."[8] They proceed to state that ethics involves more than this definition. It is "an academic discipline, a systematic set of propositions that constitute the intellectual instruments for the analysis of morality."[9] This appears to be largely a deontological definition.

The common thread here is that ethics concentrates on *human actions or on the consequences of human actions*. From a deontological perspective, ethics teaches that we ought to perform good actions, and it provides us with rules for doing so. Yet the deontological approach does not tell us *how* to do good. In a sense, the deontological approach is similar to the "twelve commandments" developed by the American Society for Public Administration for its membership. It contains rules or "moral standards," but it does not guarantee that we will follow the rules any more than the American Society for Public Administration's Code of Ethics guarantees that the membership will act in accordance with those rules.[10]

From a teleological perspective, ethics also examines human actions and their consequences—not so much by applying absolute standards or rules, but by reflecting on their meaning and determining their rightness or wrongness depending on the situation, circumstances and intention of the actor.

DIVISIONS OF ETHICS

Ethics has two parts: general ethics and special ethics. *General ethics* develops general principles concerning the morality of human actions. *Special ethics* applies the general principles developed in general ethics to people's conduct toward themselves, other human beings, society and the state. The methodology is deductive, as explained in the previous chapter.

Special ethics deduces from general principles the morality of particular, specific actions. These actions can be those of individuals, public administrators, legislators, physicians, businesspeople and the like. In arriving at the general principles, general ethics relies on experience and psychology. It sees humans as composite beings, composed of a body and a soul, endowed with speech with which to communicate and needs, some of which can be fulfilled. Through a combination of deductive reasoning and experience, ethics sees society as natural to humankind.

HUMAN ACTIONS

All these definitions of ethics suggest that it focuses on human actions and their morality. It is concerned with the morality of human behavior. But first it is important to separate human actions from their morality. The major focus of ethics is on human actions; this also happens to be the starting point for most legal systems. They are primarily interested in human actions and, following that, in their legality or illegality. Ethics, then, does not concern itself with the actions of animals. Furthermore, ethics focuses only on people's *deliberate* human actions, and not on undeliberate actions or actions done because of ignorance. The distinction here is between what philosophers call an *actus humanus* (deliberate human action) and an *actus hominis* (undeliberate action). What is it that makes an action human? What are the principal ingredients of a human action? Lawyers also focus on this issue. Deontologists use criteria to arrive at the notion of a human action while teleologists reflect on the merits of a particular action. Both may arrive at the same conclusion, but they also may not.

Scholastic philosophers maintain that three requirements must be concurrently present for any action to be human: (1) There must be some *knowledge* involved; (2) There must be *voluntariness* present; (3) The action must be *freely* done.[11] St. Thomas Aquinas discussed these three elements at length in *Summa Theologica*, Question 18.[12] If any one of these elements is not present, the action is not a human action, and therefore it is not a fitting subject for ethics.

Knowledge is an essential requirement for an action to be human. As discussed in psychology, we cannot will anything unless we first know it. So knowledge of some kind is an absolute for an action to be human.

Besides knowledge, the action must be voluntary—that is, it must proceed from the will. In chapter 3, under the discussion on psychology, the will was defined as a faculty that enables us to incline or strive after an object apprehended as good. Some actions proceed directly from the will—such as consenting—or indirectly through other faculties commanded by the will—such as thinking, seeing or walking. The will controls the performance of external actions—the will is the *cause* of our actions.[13] On the other hand, if someone places a gun in my hand and pulls the trigger, it is obvious that my will does not control or cause that action, and therefore the shooting is not voluntary and not human.

The third element in a human action is that it must be freely done. Psychology discussed in chapter 3 established that human beings have free will—that is, the capacity to act or not to act or to act in one way as opposed to another. Free will means that human beings have choices.[14] Although some human actions are voluntary, in that the actor carries out the action, not every voluntary action is free. Every free action is voluntary in that the actor without restraint carried out the action, but not every voluntary action is free. That means that while an actor may be the cause of an action, the actor was operating under conditions such as force or fear that prevented the action from being freely done. The actor was unable to exercise choice; therefore, the action, although voluntarily done, was not a free action.

The above three conditions have close connections. *Voluntariness* includes anything that proceeds from the will; therefore, it includes not only direct actions but also omissions and the effects of both actions and omissions. In addition, the actor must have some knowledge of the end or purpose of the action, omission or effect of either. This makes an action different from a mere wish or volition, which is not an action per se.

How much knowledge of the end or purpose of an action must an actor have? Scholastic philosophers argue that the actor must have "sufficient" knowledge of the end or purpose of the action for the action to be human. St. Thomas Aquinas said: "Now in order that a thing be done for an end, some knowledge of the end is necessary. . . . The voluntary is defined not only as having a principle within the agent, but also as implying knowledge."[15] For example, a dog has some knowledge of its actions. If a dog sees a bone, she probably will chase it. The dog has what philosophers call "imperfect knowledge" that makes her action a *spontaneous act*. On the other hand, if the actor lacks all knowledge of the end or purpose of his act, the action is a *natural act*. It appears that trees and plants as they grow have no knowledge of their purpose, and so the actions of growing are natural. An action is involuntary when the actor lacks all knowledge of the purpose, or acts with knowledge but not according to an act of the will. The person taking another's umbrella without knowledge illustrates this point. The action is involuntary.

Another factor involving knowledge, voluntariness and freedom is the distinction between what is directly voluntary and what is voluntary in cause. An action is *directly voluntary* when the actor wills the action for himself or as a means to an end. A student can will to take a course in public administration or will to obtain an MPA, which makes a particular course a means to earning an MPA. On the other hand, *voluntary in cause* means that the action is not directly willed for its own sake but arises from another action directly willed. An action is voluntary in cause if the actor foresees that it will result from another action directly willed. For example, a fighter pilot may directly will the dropping of bombs over a military target, but may see indirectly that the action (bombing a military target) may result in killing innocent civilians. The latter action may be voluntary in cause, depending on what the pilot foresaw at the time of his direct actions. The test here is what the actor foresaw. In reality, it makes little difference whether the act is voluntary now (direct) or voluntary because of a previously willed action (voluntary in cause) because of foresight. The same principle applies to an action done with reluctance or only because of circumstances. The test again is what the actor foresaw at the time of the action. In practice, voluntary-in-cause actions tend to be less voluntary than actions directly willed.[16]

IMPEDIMENTS TO HUMAN ACTION

This discussion limits the number of actions performed by human beings that can genuinely be human actions. If any of the three conditions is absent, the action is not human and is not subject to examination in ethics. Civil law, however, may not treat the action the same way. Prosecuting attorneys tend to see *all* actions as human actions, and therefore subject to the scrutiny of the law. Defense attorneys, on the other hand, tend to show that actions of defendants were not human actions and therefore the defendant is not culpable. The three criteria imply that there may be other factors that render actions nonhuman and therefore not subject to scrutiny in ethics. There are several such factors, some of which St. Thomas Aquinas addressed.[17]

Ignorance

Since knowledge is an important requirement in assessing whether an action is human or not, it is obvious that factors interfering with knowledge also interfere with whether an action is human. The first such factor is ignorance. Ignorance is the absence of knowledge in a subject capable of having knowledge, or lack of knowledge in a subject who should have knowledge. An animal cannot be ignorant because of its inability to have human knowledge. But a public manager can be ignorant if she lacks knowledge of managerial principles or ethics in public organizations.

Several types of ignorance have ramifications on whether actions are human or not. The first is the distinction between *ignorance of law* and *ignorance of fact*. In the first case, the actor is ignorant—does not know—that the law exists. Legal prosecutors tend to argue that once the lawful authority promulgates a law, we must presume that subjects are aware of the existence of that law. Therefore, ignorance of the law is a myth. But in ethics, ignorance of the existence of the law through no fault of the actor does diminish the humanness of the action; if the actor violates the law through such ignorance, the action is not a human action. Ignorance of fact, on the other hand, means that the actor is aware of the existence of the law but uncertain or ignorant about the nature of his action or the circumstances in which he is operating—the actor is unsure that his action is violating the law. If there is no doubt in the actor's mind that the action, which actually is a violation of the law, is not a violation of the law, that particular action does not violate the law. A court of law may see the same action differently, but ethics is not just law—it is broader than the law.

A more critical element of ignorance is the distinction between invincible and vincible ignorance. *Invincible ignorance* means that the actor does not even suspect that she is ignorant or that she is in doubt about the nature of the action but does not have access through common sense to dispel the doubt. *Vincible ignorance*, on the other hand, means that the actor can through the use of ordinary care or common sense dispel the doubt.

Invincible ignorance destroys the voluntariness of an action. The actor does not know or cannot know the truth about his action, and so invincible ignorance destroys one essential ingredient of a human action—knowledge. Actions done through invincible ignorance are not human actions, and the actors are not responsible for the consequences of these actions. (Courts of law may take a different view of these actions.)

Vincible ignorance does not destroy voluntariness because the actor in these circumstances adverts to her ignorance and does not take sufficient steps to dispel the ignorance. Such a person must accept the consequences of the action. An action performed because of vincible ignorance is voluntary in cause and, as stated above, tends to lessen voluntariness or make the actor less responsible than if she directly willed the action.

Passion

Passions influence human action. Psychology studies human passions in detail. Passions are powerful emotions or appetites springing from a pretense of something perceived as good or evil; they are usually accompanied by bodily changes. Passions include human appetites, such as anger, grief, love, hatred or greed. Thus a grieving person often sheds tears and makes grieving sounds.

Some passions precede an act of the will and cause the will to act. Sometimes, the actor deliberately arouses his passions. If the passions that precede an action are not deliberately aroused, such as a sudden rage or a fit of anger, they help to increase the onward movement of the will to act, but simultaneously diminish the freedom of the will. The action is still a human action to the extent that freedom of the will can be measured. If, on the other hand, we do not cause a particular passion and that passion destroys the use of reason, it also destroys the voluntariness of the action and thus renders it an *actus hominis*.

When an actor deliberately arouses a passion before acting, it is obvious that the voluntary nature of the action also increases. If that passion should destroy the use of reason, the deliberate arousal of the passion is a direct action and any subsequent action is voluntary in cause or an effect of causing the passion to emerge. An example is a person deliberately causing herself to become enraged, and as a result killing another person. The killing is voluntary in cause and the actor is guilty of homicide to the extent that she foresaw the killing.

Fear

Fear may influence human action to the extent of rendering it non-human, somewhat human or totally human. Fear is mental trepidation or an emotional reaction arising from an impending danger. There are two kinds of fear: (1) grave fear, or that which would affect a person of ordinary courage in the same circumstances; (2) light fear, or that which would not affect a person of ordinary courage in the same situation. Fear may come from sources outside ourselves for from within. It can be inflicted justly or unjustly—justly when inflicted by a person with the right to inflict it and in the proper manner, as happens when a judge acts; or unjustly when inflicted either by a person without authority or in an improper manner.

The principle governing fear is that whatever fear (usually grave fear) is so strong as to destroy a person's freedom of choice also destroys the voluntariness of that action. The action is not a human action. If the fear (usually light fear) does not destroy the person's freedom but only diminishes it, the subsequent action is voluntary in proportion to the amount of liberty the person had.

Violence

Violence can influence the degree to which actions are human or not. Violence is external physical force exerted on a person. When a person offers all the resistance he can, actions done in these circumstances are unfree and therefore not human actions. If he does not offer as much resistance as possible, the actions performed may be less free and so human in proportion to the resistance not exerted.

Habit

Habit can influence the nature of human action. Habit is a quality acquired through frequent repetition that enables the subject to act easily and promptly. It is an inclination that is also difficult to remove. Good habits are virtues and bad habits are vices. The issue here is the influence of habits on voluntariness. That a person acquires a habit shows voluntariness at work. But when we acquire habits our individual actions, such as smoking, may become less voluntary because of a lack of advertence to a particular action. However, if a person acquiring a habit foresees the results, good or bad, that does not lessen the voluntariness of subsequent actions. These actions are at least voluntary in cause and are subject to the same assessment.

Temperament

Temperament may influence voluntariness. Temperament is the sum of a person's natural propensities as opposed to character, which is the collection of a person's acquired propensities, such as habits. Temperament and character may sometimes lessen the voluntariness of actions, but never destroy it.

Pathological States

There are many pathological states that may interfere with voluntariness, in that they blur knowledge and weaken the will. In criminal cases, attorneys pay great attention to these mental states. Amentia, or arrested mental development caused by injury or disease, and dementia, or disorder in a once developed mind, clearly affect the voluntariness of human actions because they impair knowledge.

Insanity, psychoneurosis, psychosis, schizophrenia and the like may also impact on the voluntariness of human actions. But there is always a question of whether these conditions sufficiently removed human reason to render the action nonhuman. It may be commonplace to plead insanity in murder trials, but the ethics of the actions focuses solely on how much knowledge and reason the actor had when the murder was done.

Another issue is sleep walking. If a sleepwalker kills another person or commits a crime, is he guilty and to what extent? From what has been said, if the sleepwalker is completely asleep and lacks all knowledge, voluntariness or freedom, the action is not a human action; it falls into the *actus hominis* category. So it is not an action that ethics can judge. However, if there were some reason or knowledge involved, ethics would assess the nature of the action based on that factor.

Other conditions that impact on the voluntariness of human actions include drugs and alcohol. These substances can impair human reasoning and knowledge. Many people raise the issue of the guilt or innocence of the intoxicated person who, while driving home after drinking, kills an innocent person. Is this person guilty of both drunkenness and murder? The answer goes back to the distinction between direct voluntariness and voluntary in cause. It depends on what the intoxicated person foresaw at the time of her drinking. It is a question of what that person knew at the time, not before starting to drink and not afterward.

SUMMARY

This chapter has focused on definitions of ethics and particularly on human actions as the starting point of ethics. It should be clear that the conditions involved in defining human actions limit the number of actions that come under the scrutiny of ethics. While civil law may look on both human actions and *actus hominum* as legitimate targets for scrutiny under the law, ethics limits its view to solely human actions. If the action is not human, ethics does not consider the action from a moral perspective. The next chapter focuses on the morality of human actions.

NOTES

1. William K. Frankena, *Ethics* (Englewood Cliffs, N.J.: Prentice-Hall, 1963). Also, Daniel Callahan and H. Tristram Englehardt, *The Roots of Ethics—Science, Religion, and Values* (New York: Plenum Press, 1981).

2. Cyril L. Means, *The Ethical Imperative* (New York: Anchor Books, 1970).

3. W. T. Jones, *Approaches to Ethics: Representative Selections from Classical Times to the Present*, Third Edition (New York: McGraw-Hill, 1977).

4. Winter Gibson, *Elements for a Social Ethic: The Role of Social Sciences in Public Policy* (New York: Macmillan, 1966), pp. 124–41.

5. James M. Gustafson, *Theology and Christian Ethics*. Philadelphia: United Church Press, 1974.

6. Cynthia J. McSwain, and Orion F. White, Jr., "The Case of Lying, Cheating, and Stealing—Personal Development as Ethical Guidance for Managers," *Administration and Society* 18, no. 4 (February 1987).

7. Jeremy Bentham, *The Principles of Morals and Legislation* (New York: Hofner, 1948), pp. 311–12.

8. Albert R. Jonsen and Andre E. Hellegers, "Conceptual Foundations for an Ethics of Medical Care," in *Ethics for Health Care*, Lawrence R. Tancredi, ed. (Washington, D.C.: National Academy of Sciences, 1974), p. 4.

9. Ibid., p. 4.

10. "Code of Ethics," American Society for Public Administration, Washington, D.C., April 8, 1984.

11. Anton Pegis, ed., *Basic Writings of Saint Thomas Aquinas*, Volume One (New York: Random House, 1945), pp. 317–33.

12. Anton Pegis, ed., *Basic Writings of Saint Thomas Anquinas*, Volume Two (New York: Random House, 1945), pp. 777–85.

13. Ibid., Vol. Two, pp. 786–92.

14. Ibid., pp. 226–27.

15. Ibid., pp. 228–30.

16. Ibid., pp. 230–38.

17. Ibid., pp. 232–38.

CHAPTER 5

The Morality of Human Action

DEFINITION OF MORALITY

Ethics focuses not only on human action but also on its morality. Once we decide that an action is human, then that action becomes subject matter for ethics. It is an important function of ethics to figure out whether particular human actions are moral or not. Morality involves the examination of human action to decide if it is good, bad or indifferent—to figure out if it is right or wrong, good or bad.

Psychology has established that humans have free will. People have the capacity to choose one action and reject another. People have the capacity to choose what is right and reject what is wrong or vice versa. Free will plays a vital role in human action and in its morality.

Ontology involves the nature of causality, the difference between cause and effect and the Principle of Sufficient Reason. Epistemology further elaborated on judgments arrived at by generalization. By combining these two studies we can say that if we know the nature or purpose of something or some being, we can fairly accurately decide what kinds of activities are good or bad for that particular thing. For example, if we know what the nature or purpose of a knife is, we can fairly accurately figure out what activities are good or bad for a knife so that it can achieve its purpose. If we know what activities a being does, we can fairly accurately decide the purpose of that being.

Based on this approach, we can say that a thing is good when it is in harmony with or fits a nature. Rightness involves the means to an end—an action is right when it fits a particular end. To decide the morality of human actions, ethics must first determine the end or purpose of human actions— the ultimate end of these actions. *End* or *purpose* means the reason for which a person performs an action. Some human actions can have many and different purposes, including immediate and ultimate ones.[1] Scholars have different views of what constitutes the ultimate purpose of human actions.

THE PURPOSE OF HUMAN ACTION

Epicureans, discussed in chapter 2, held that humankind's happiness consists in obtaining all the pleasure that life can offer. The ultimate purpose of human action is pleasure. This is the "eat, drink and be merry" code of ethics.

Another group of philosophers, the Stoics, claimed that the highest good a human can acquire is the cultivation of the mind or control over knowledge. Humans can attain perfect knowledge in this life; the ultimate purpose of human action is to cultivate the human mind or acquire knowledge.

Materialism or communism maintains that people's happiness consists in acquiring material goods. The acquisition of wealth is or should be the ultimate purpose of human action.

Humanism holds that the ultimate end of human action is in achieving prosperity and progress for the human race. This is equivalent to the theory of economic plenty. Other forms of humanism are narrower, in that they see the ultimate end of human action as achieving prosperity and progress for a nation. This can lead to extreme nationalism. Humanitarianism sees the ultimate end of human action as service, whether it be service to humankind in general, to a nation, to an organization or to a group. The highest good people can achieve is to serve.

Scholastics base their theory of the ultimate end of human actions on philosophy. From theodicy, they claim that a supreme being exists and that humans ultimately depend on and can be completely satisfied only by association with the supreme being.[2] From psychology they claim that humans are composed of a body and a spiritual soul, and the spiritual soul is the link with the supreme being. Only something that is all good (excluding evil), desirable and perpetual can satisfy people's insatiable appetite for happiness. No created goods (goods of the body, mind or material) can completely satisfy these appetites after which the human will strives, as psychology establishes.[3] Scholastics argue that, while beginning to attain the perfect good starts in this life, perfect beatitude does not occur until another life or a life after death. Psychology establishes that a person's soul continues to exist after death, and perfect beatitude ultimately rests with a person's soul in a future life of association with the supreme being.

Chapter 2 suggested that we can consider human action from various points of view. Physiology considers the physical makeup of human action. Psychology focuses on the activities of the mind, as does epistemology. Ethics examines the purpose of action, especially ultimate end. Finally, *morality* is the conformity or lack of conformity of a human action with the actor's purpose. Morality is the relationship of action to purpose; it is a quality applied to human action, as discussed earlier in this chapter.

THE DIFFERENCE BETWEEN MORAL GOOD AND MORAL EVIL

The same physical action may at different times be morally good or morally evil. For example, driving through a red light may be morally evil. But if authorities remove the light, the same physical act of driving through the intersection may be morally good. What makes the difference between a morally good action and a morally evil one? Does the difference rest in some extrinsic circumstance, such as a law or a red light, or in some intrinsic circumstance or nature of the action itself? The fundamental question is, Are all human actions right or wrong because of some extrinsic circumstances, such as rules of law, or are at least some human actions *intrinsically evil*? There are different schools of thought on this point.

Divine positivists claim that actions are good or evil only because God has freely commanded them to be so. They say God, who has forbidden lying, could just as easily have forbidden telling the truth. Positive laws of God determine the morality of human actions, therefore these theorists are *divine positivists*.

The problem with this theory is that it is difficult to comprehend how God could command murder to be right and moral at one time and at another time to be immoral or evil. This is contrary to the common experience of people of all times and of all places, who have determined that murder is evil. If the divine positivist position is correct, ethics serves no useful purpose because human reason is incapable of distinguishing between right and wrong—only God can do that.

Human positivists, on the other hand, hold that the difference between right and wrong arose from tribal custom or because of education or social influences. Jean-Jacques Rousseau held that actions are good when the state commands them and evil when the state forbids them. He was an evolutionary positivist. Thomas Huxley taught that the notions of moral good and moral evil have changed. Polygamy among the Jewish people was once lawful and moral, but today it is immoral.

It is true that education and cultural development help clarify our perception of what is right and wrong. They provide a better understanding of ethics. But education and cultural development alone cannot explain the universal agreement that certain actions, such as murder, are morally evil.

Scholastic philosophers maintain that there is an intrinsic difference between good and evil. They say that at least some human actions are *intrinsically evil and some actions are intrinsically good.* According to the scholastics, actions that lead a man toward his end are good and actions that lead a man away from his end are evil. There are actions of both kinds. Therefore some actions are intrinsically good and others are intrinsically evil, with an intrinsic difference between good and evil.[4]

In support of this position, the scholastics point to these universal judgments that some actions are morally right and others are morally wrong. While these philosophers cannot agree on the morality of all actions, or perhaps on much of anything else, they have agreed that some actions such as murder, robbery or treachery are morally wrong by their very nature. They may not agree on the number and kind of human actions that fit into the intrinsic evil category. For example, Patrick Buchanan, in the *Washington Times*, said: "Cardinal O'Connor has done nothing but assert Catholic doctrine on homosexuality and abortion; i.e., both are intrinsically wrong."[5] Although Buchanan cited the Bible and not ethics as the source of his claim, he illustrates the point made here that sometimes at least there is an intrinsic difference between a good action and an evil action. But how does a person decide the difference between the two? What constitutes the essence of morality?

THE ESSENCE OF MORALITY

Morality concerns the fundamental reason why some actions are good and others are evil. It is a test to find out what acts are good and what acts are evil. It is a search for criteria to assess the goodness or badness of human action. There are several schools of thought on this issue.

Utilitarianism

Utilitarians claim that the test of goodness or badness of a human action is the usefulness of the action. This is largely a teleological theory. An action is morally good if it is useful and morally evil if it is not.

There are two kinds of utilitarians, who differ only on the notion of usefulness. Individual utilitarianism, or hedonism, originated with Epicurus and is discussed in chapter 2. It also was popular in France during the nineteenth century. It holds that an action is intrinsically good if it is useful for or brings pleasure to the individual. An action is morally evil if it destroys or diminishes a person's pleasure. Actions that initially bring pleasure but subsequently bring pain or punishment are good or evil according to their most pronounced effect. For example, a person drinking alcohol may derive certain pleasure, but a subsequent hangover may bring pain or driving-while-intoxicated arrest may result in punishment. The most pronounced effect determines the morality of the action of drinking alcohol.

Social utilitarianism, or altruism, holds that an action is morally good if it is useful for the community: the greatest good for the greatest number. Actions are good or evil inasfar as they advance or hinder the happiness or good of the community. Advocates of this theory include John Stuart Mill and Jeremy Bentham, discussed in chapter 2.

Herbert Spencer combined these two theories. He stated that an action is good if it brings pleasure to the individual and simultaneously promotes the good of the community. Actions are good if they increase life, but evil if they decrease life. Spencer admitted there may be conflicts between what is good for the individual and what is good for the community, because we have not yet evolved sufficiently to achieve perfect harmony between the individual and the community. Until the human race has sufficiently evolved, we must compromise, deciding the morality of the actions involved.

The main criticism of utilitarianism in general is that it often promotes selfishness. It also assumes without proof that people can satisfy their needs for the perpetual good in their lives. Individual utilitarianism provides no advance guarantee that an action will bring pleasure or pain; often a person must act before experiencing pleasure or pain. If pleasure is the sole criterion of moral goodness, every act, including stealing, murder, and so on, can be moral. The same argument applies to social utilitarianism—that is, every act done for the good of the community is moral. Social utilitarianism also destroys the dignity of the individual and makes people cogs in the wheel of human progress.

Intuitionism

Intuitionism claims we know that ethical principles are valid and universal by intuition. Human beings have a special sense faculty that enables them to perceive directly what is right and what is wrong. Just as human beings have a sense of taste by which they can distinguish what is bitter from what is sweet, so too they have a moral faculty to enable them to distinguish what is right from what is wrong. What brings pleasure to this moral faculty is good and what brings displeasure is evil. Another version of intuitionism claims that the ultimate criterion of morality is common sense. People have principles that they form instinctively but cannot explain. These principles enable them to instinctively or intuitively feel what is good or what is evil.

The main problem with intuitionism is that it attempts only to tell us how we know *what* is good and not *what* is good. It offers no proof that we have a moral faculty or instinct that tells us what is right and what is wrong. It is true that human beings have consciences, but consciences do not work automatically and are not instincts.

Rationalism

Moral rationalism is the theory of Immanuel Kant, discussed in chapters 2 and 3. It is a deontological theory. Kant disagreed with the two theories just discussed. He claimed that no action is moral if it is done for pleasure or any other motive than duty or respect for the law. In practical reasoning, human beings have among the twelve *a priori* gates what Kant called the Categorical Imperative. This Categorical Imperative orders a person to do good and avoid evil. Acts are good or bad as out of respect for the Categorical Imperative or not. An act is good according to the motive of the actor; the only motive that makes an act good is respect for duty or law. Acts are good, according to Kant, if they can be universalized—that is, we should act in the way everybody else in the same circumstances would act. The essential element in determining morality is human reason. Thus, the ultimate test of goodness or badness of human actions is the Categorical Imperative of practical reason.

The criticism of Kant's theories in chapters 2 and 3 applies here. There is no evidence that the Categorical Imperative exists. If it does exist, it would not explain the morality of actions taken when no law exists to command such actions. Kant's canonization of human reason as the sole and infallible interpreter of morality is flawed, as the philosophical theories discussed here and in chapters 2 and 3 attest.

Scholasticism

Scholastic philosophers maintain that the essence of morality lies in human nature considered in its totality—that is, in all its parts and all its relationships, including those with other human beings, the universe and the supreme being. Human beings have a rational nature, as psychology established. Once we know the nature of something, we can come to know its purpose and what will help it to attain it. For humans, it is proximately a rational nature that determines what is good and what is bad. Borrowing from theodicy, the scholastics go one step further and argue that the decision on the morality of human action rests with the supreme being, on whom humans ultimately depend.[6]

The criteria for assessing the morality of human action are a fundamental issue that has intrigued philosophers. Philosophers have focused on and put forward several different criteria for assessing morality, but a single criterion of pleasure and the existence of a Categorical Imperative are insufficient explanations of morality. Scholastic theory is more comprehensive. It considers several criteria, including the body and soul, the intellect and senses, human relationships with various entities and the circumstances in which humans find themselves. It is reasonable to consider all elements in determining what is right and what is wrong. Both the deontological and teleological schools of thought probably concur on this point. Yet the teleological school might consider departing from this theory if it limits the application of criteria to an action before commission, as opposed to concomitant or subsequent application.

DETERMINANTS OF MORALITY

What parts of a human action should we examine to decide if the action concurs with human nature, as discussed in the previous section? There are three parts to every action that we should examine: the object of the action, the circumstances in which the action was performed and the end or purpose of the act. Sometimes these three components are the only practical criteria a public administrator will have to decide the morality of a public action.[7] Essentially this is the basis of the teleological approach.

Object of a Human Action

The object of an action is the first part of any action in a morality assessment. The object of any action is its essence.[8] It is that which makes an action be what it is and not something else. Every action has an object. The object distinguishes the act from every other act. That object can be something good, bad or indifferent—that is, neither good nor bad. Lying and telling the truth are examples of two actions that are distinguished from each other according to moral criteria. The following principles apply to the object of every action.

1. An action whose object is bad by its very nature will remain bad and nothing can improve it—neither circumstances, nor purpose, nor intention. A lie, defined as speaking contrary to what is in the speaker's mind, remains a lie despite the purpose or circumstance involved. Purpose and circumstance do not make it anything (another object) except a lie.

2. An action that is good may become bad because of circumstances or purpose. For example, telling the truth is a good act. By telling the truth, when silence would suffice, to destroy another person's good name or character makes the good act of telling the truth a morally bad act because of the speaker's purpose or intention.

3. An action that is indifferent (neither good nor bad) may become good or bad because of circumstances or purpose. Walking may be an indifferent act. But walking into a store to steal becomes a morally evil action because of the purpose.

Circumstances of a Human Action

Circumstances are those qualities that make an abstract act concrete and individual. Circumstances include such things as the act being done at a particular time, in a particular place, by a particular agent, in a particular manner. Moral circumstances, not physical, are the criteria for assessing the goodness or badness of a human action.[9] Moral circumstances may increase the goodness or badness of a human action. To strike another person in self-defense is one thing; to strike another without any provocation or justification is another matter.

Some moral circumstances are aggravating when they increase the goodness or badness of an action. Thus, stealing from a homeless person is an *aggravating* circumstance that increases the badness of an already bad act. Circumstances are *extenuating* when they decrease the amount of badness of an action. For example, to steal $10 from the Chase Manhattan Bank is not as bad as stealing $10 from a homeless person, but it is still an evil act. Moral circumstances are *specifying* when they make an indifferent act become good or bad, or when they give a new kind of goodness or badness to an action. For example, taking money from a till is an indifferent act. If the money belongs to the taker, the act is all right. But if the money belongs to another person, it is an evil, immoral act.

Some philosophers maintain that circumstances are the sole criterion for judging the morality of a human action. Joseph Fletcher, in particular, reflected this position.[10] To a certain extent, subscribers to the teleological theory (interpretivists) may appear to focus more closely on the circumstances of an action, to the extent that they strive to understand or give meaning to a human action. However, interpretivists need not limit their consideration of morality to mere circumstances; they also can, as stated above, consider the nature of the action and its purpose.

The most difficult problem in situation ethics is that it often makes morality subjective and relative. There is nothing to prevent two persons in same circumstances from giving two diametrically opposite meanings to the same action. This implies that an action that is morally good for one person is morally evil for another. Although interpretivists do subscribe to human reason as an interpreter of human actions, the person who focuses on the situation alone cannot be sure of the moralitiy of at least some actions.

The End or Purpose of a Human Action

The end of a human action is the purpose the person had in mind while doing the act. It is the intention. People can have only one purpose or have a variety of purposes in doing a particular act.[11] We can deduce certain principles based on the purpose in mind when performing the act.

1. An action that is indifferent because of its object may become good or bad because of the purpose. For example, jogging in itself is an indifferent act. When done to maintain good health, it becomes a good act. When done to arrive at a place where the person commits theft or murder, it becomes an immoral action.

2. An action that is good because of its object may become more good or less good or even bad because of the purpose. For example, to give a donation to a homeless person is a good action. If you give the donation just to get rid of the person, it is still a good action, but not as good as in the first case. If you give the donation to lure the homeless person into doing something evil or immoral for you, the donation becomes an immoral act.

3. An action that is evil by its object may become more wrong or perhaps less wrong, but never good by its purpose. For instance, telling a lie is morally wrong. But telling a lie to defame another person is more wrong. Telling a lie "to get out of trouble" or to protect the interests of another person is still lying and still wrong, but less wrong because of the purpose. A good end does not justify a bad means.

THE CONSEQUENCES OF MORAL ACTIONS

The foregoing discussion attributed morality to human actions—that is, actions over which the actor has control. A consequence of these factors is that moral acts are imputed to the doer. The effects of an action are attributable to the doer as the cause of the act. When the actor physically does the act, the action is physically imputed to that person—the person is responsible for his or her action.[12] If the actor does not perform the act but causes another to do it, the first person is still morally responsible for the consequences of the act to the degree that he or she foresaw those consequences. Whatever increases, lessens or destroys the liberty and knowledge that are essential for a moral act also increases, lessens or destroys the responsibility of the actor. On the other hand, the actions of other people may be imputed to us if we have helped, encouraged or persuaded them to do something or if we have remained silent when these people clearly needed advice.

When are we responsible for the effect of our actions? To be responsible for an evil effect we must advert at least vaguely to the fact that the action is bad. If we so advert, we are presumed to have willed the effect. For example, a hunter sees an object but is unsure whether it is a man or a deer. The hunter adverts at least vaguely to what the consequences of firing a shot may be. The hunter shoots anyhow, and therefore the presumption is that the hunter willed the effect of his action. On the other hand, for a good effect to be imputed, the actor must advert to the good effect and intend it. For example, after a presentation by a speaker on government travel regulations, a member of the audience decides to reimburse the government for overreimbursement. If the speaker never considered—much less intended—the good effect, the speaker is not responsible for it.

ACTS OF DOUBLE EFFECT

Some actions have two effects—good and bad. How does someone decide the morality of such actions? Ethicists provide a few general principles to help decide the morality of acts of double effect. They are:

1. The action that produces the two effects must be either good or indifferent—that is, not intrinsically wrong.
2. The good effect must be immediate—that is, not obtained through the evil effect.
3. The intention or purpose must be good.
4. There must be a proportionately good reason or cause for performing the action in the first place.

The most difficult problem with acts of double effect is to figure out whether the evil effect caused the good effect. One way of resolving this problem is by asking the following question: If you take away the evil effect, does the good effect remain? If the good effect remains, the evil effect did not cause it. If there is doubt and it appears that the good effect also disappears, it is important to discover if the good effect has been unduly subordinated to the evil effect.

Acts of double effect are of great interest to most people. They often cite the example of the pregnant woman about to deliver, whose physician has diagnosed serious medical complications. In the physician's opinion, it may not be possible to save both lives. Many have claimed that this example allows the physician "to kill the mother to save the baby." Others have said that the physician may "kill the baby to save the mother."

Examples of this kind are somewhat rare. Every physician will do his or her utmost to save both lives. But if, finally, it is a question of one life versus the other, the following principle holds. *It is lawful (moral) to perform an act of two effects (one life saved, the other lost) provided the actor (physician) intends the good effect although the actor forsees that the evil effect is possible and perhaps probable.* The actor does not intend the evil effect. In the case of the pregnant woman, the physician may perform a surgical procedure intending to save the woman's life (good effect), but from which procedure the physician foresees that death of the unborn infant (evil effect) will result. However, the physician does not intend this evil effect.

The good purpose—saving the pregnant woman's life—is the primary effect, and the physician does not intend the foreseen and probable evil effect. This principle may not seem to comply with the condition that the good effect is not obtained through the evil effect, but on reflection it does. If we remove the evil effect—the death of the fetus—the good effect remains. The surgical procedure is not the evil effect; it is an indifferent act, neither good nor bad in itself. But the surgical procedure causes two effects, one that the physician intends and the other he or she does not intend.

There are several actions that potentially have double effects. One is hunger strike, sometimes embarked upon to secure a country's liberty and independence but with possible death of the striker foreseen. Police officers often encounter situations of double effect, where their primary mission is to save people in danger but foresee the potential loss of their own lives. Military fighter pilots encounter situations of double effect in times of war. Likewise, public administrators and politicians too frequently find themselves confronted by circumstances where their actions may result in double effects. Often there are no laws or regulations on what to do, except the nature of the action, the circumstances in which they find themselves and their action's purpose.

Laws and regulations provide important guidance to all public administrators in determining what is ethical or moral. The next chapter focuses on these laws and regulations. Every person, too, has a conscience, and the next chapter also considers what conscience is and how it applies the principles outlined in this chapter, as well as the principles of law, to every human action.

NOTES

1. Anton C. Pegis, *Basic Writings of Saint Thomas Aquinas*, Volume Two (New York: Random House, 1945), p. 274.

2. Ibid., pp. 84–87, 359–65.

3. Ibid., pp. 257–58, 84ff.

4. Ibid., p. 318.

5. *Washington Times*, December 18, 1989. "The Desecration of St. Patrick's."

6. Pegis, *Basic Writings of Saint Thomas Aquinas*, pp. 228–29.

7. Ibid., p. 322. See also Albert R. Jonsen and Andre E. Hellegers, "Conceptual Foundations for a Ethics of Medical Care," in *Ethics for Health Care*, Laurence R. Tancredi, ed. (Washington, D.C.: National Academy of Sciences, 1974), pp. 10–11.

8. Pegis, *Basic Writings of Saint Thomas Aquinas*, pp. 319–20.

9. Ibid., pp. 320–21.

10. Joseph Fletcher, *Situation Ethics: The New Morality* (New York: Westminster, 1966).

11. Pegis, *Basic Writings of Saint Thomas Aquinas*, pp. 274–75.

12. Ibid., pp. 359–65.

CHAPTER 6

Laws, Rules, Regulations and Conscience as Sources of Ethical Guidance

The two previous chapters examined the meaning of human action and criteria for judging morality. There are two other sources of guidance from a deontological perspective by which human beings can judge the morality of their actions. These sources are particularly important to public administrators and may offer clearer and more practical guidance. One is outside the actor, and is law; the second is within the actor, and is conscience. These two impose on us an obligation to be moral—that is, to do good and avoid evil. This chapter examines law and conscience as sources of ethical guidance. It provides a theoretical framework for ethical guidance based on laws, rules, regulations and conscience.

THE NOTION OF LAW

Law as used here is different from the notion of law in physics, which implies a common or constant way of action. In ethics, law has a moral connotation. St. Thomas Aquinas defined law as "an ordinance of reason for the common good, promulgated by him who has care of the community."[1] Aquinas explained that the word *lex* (Latin for "law") comes from the Latin word *ligare*, which means "to bind." It induces people to act or restrains them from acting.[2] It imposes an obligation.

Law, then, sets up a course of action that must be followed. St. Thomas Aquinas said that, in drawing up a course of action, the legislator must act reasonably. What the legislator commands must be good, possible and just. Laws must conform to human nature. It must be physically and morally possible to obey the laws. Laws must also be just, distributing goods and burdens equally. The law is for common, not private, good. Before anyone can be expected to obey a law, the legislator must promulgate it or make it known to the community. If the legislator does not promulgate or publicize the existence of a law, citizens will be ignorant of its existence and the legislator cannot expect obedience.[3]

Although law is an ordinance or a rule resulting from human reason, it is not the same as a regulation or ordinary rule. Regulations often help clarify laws, although sometimes they do not achieve that objective. Regulations focus on the individual good, whereas the purpose of a law is to promote the common good. On the basis of *source*, the authority to enact a law belongs to those with jurisdiction or those who are lawfully in charge of the community. The source of a regulation is any private authority, such as an organization, a superior or a head of household. On the basis of *extent*, a law does not ordinarily bind outside the territory of the legislator. U.S. laws do not bind in Europe,[4] whereas a regulation may bind a person wherever he or she goes. In the presidential primary of 1992, candidate Bill Clinton noted this distinction when asked if he ever used drugs. He said that he never broke any laws of the United States by using drugs. Later, when asked if he broke any laws anywhere by using drugs, he admitted to having used marijuana once as a student at Oxford University in England. He was thereby claiming that the laws of the United States do not bind a U.S. citizen in England.

In spite of the foregoing distinction, an interesting development occurred in Ireland during the spring of 1992. A fourteen-year-old Irish girl became pregnant as a result of an alleged rape. She and her parents went to England to procure an abortion, which the Irish Constitution prohibits in Ireland. The Irish attorney general brought the matter before the High Court in Dublin. The Court decided that the Irish Constitution barred the fourteen-year-old from having an abortion elsewhere in England. The Supreme Court of Ireland reviewed this decision on appeal; however, it did not rule, as most scholars expected, that the young woman had the constitutional right to travel to England to have an abortion. Rather, it ruled that she could obtain an abortion on the grounds that she was threatening suicide. Her right to life took precedence over the right to life of the fetus.

It appears that, at least in this incident, the Irish courts consider the law—the Irish Constitution—to apply beyond Ireland, at least in instances where pregnancy termination is concerned. According to the Irish Courts, the right to travel—a right to which all members of the European Community, including Ireland, subscribe—is secondary to the right to life. The courts have left it to the legislative process in Ireland to clarify these issues.

But we can seriously question how an Irish law or the Irish Constitution can bind an Irish citizen living either legally or illegally in the United States. Many Irish Americans have dual citizenship, yet have never set foot in Ireland. It is difficult to comprehend how the Irish Constitution or the Irish laws can bind them.[5]

DIVISIONS OF LAW

St. Thomas Aquinas provided a famous description of the various kinds of law. The diagram below provides a graphic view of his description.[6] I include this here primarily as an overview of the concept of law. Aquinas distinguished between *eternal law* derived from theodicy, which shows God as the ruler of the universe, and *eternal law*, with temporal law or laws passed in time (see Figure 2). Two kinds of law exist in time—natural law and positive law. Natural law developed with time or with the coming of human beings. It is based on human nature, and human reason can discover it. Positive law also developed with time. It consists of laws that depend on the free will of the legislators and are promulgated by some external sign. There are two kinds of positive laws—divine and human. If the author of the positive laws is God, they are divine positive laws. If the immediate source of a positive law is human, it is a human positive law. In addition, there are two types of divine positive laws—the Old and New Testaments. There are two kinds of human positive laws—civil if enacted by the state and canon if passed and promulgated by the church. Here I focus on natural law and positive, human civil law.

Figure 2
Divisions of Law

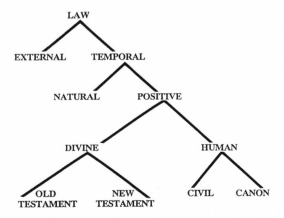

Natural Law

The Senate hearings in the fall of 1991 to confirm Judge Clarence Thomas as an associate justice of the U.S. Supreme Court produced considerable debate on natural law. Senator Joseph Biden, in particular, questioned Judge Thomas on his views of natural law vis-à-vis the U.S. Constitution. Speculation arose as to whether it was appropriate for a Supreme Court Justice to go beyond the U.S. Constitution to natural law in interpreting the Constitution. The debate seemed to imply that while natural law is the ultimate criterion governing human conduct, it is relatively clear and easy to discover.

Definition of Natural Law

What is natural law? St. Thomas Aquinas defined natural law as "participation of the eternal law in the rational creature."[7] To arrive at this definition, he discussed eternal law as God's overall plan for the universe, including inanimate objects. He confined natural law to human beings or rational creatures. Natural law is "an imprint on us of the divine light."[8] This parallels the definition of St. Paul in his famous letter to the Romans. He says natural law is written in the hearts of men: "When the Gentiles who have no law do by nature what the law prescribes, these having no law a law unto themselves. They show the work of the law written in their hearts. Their conscience bears witness to them, even when conflicting thoughts accuse or defend them" (Rom. 1:14–15).[9]

Does a natural law exist? There are strong *a priori* and *a posteriori* arguments to suggest it does. One *a posteriori* argument, or an argument based on human experience, is as follows: It is a fact that people of all times and in all places regardless of the degree of civilization reached, have distinguished between right and wrong actions. They have also agreed that human beings should be good and avoid evil. These universal beliefs suggest that people *by nature* form these moral judgments. The formation of these moral judgments suggests that a natural law exists or that it is embedded in human nature.

Qualities of Natural Law

According to St. Thomas Aquinas, natural law has two qualities: universality and immutability. *Universality* means that natural law extends to all human beings. The argument from experience in the previous paragraph suggests so. All human beings have the same human reason and can have at least some knowledge of what is right and what is wrong. But natural law may not manifest itself in the same way to all human beings.

St. Thomas Aquinas distinguished among first, second, and third principles of natural law.[10] First, or primary, principles are universal rules of conduct that all human beings can easily know by use of reason. These rules are immediately evident and include doing good, avoiding evil, living reasonably, and so on. Human beings have a natural inclination to doing good and avoiding evil—or to what is perceived as good or evil. All other principles are based on and derived from these first principles.

Secondary principles are those easily deduced from primary principles. A person with normal understanding cannot be ignorant of them except through vincible ignorance. For example, if natural law prescribes doing good, then respect for one's parents, family or other human beings must be a good thing.

Tertiary principles of natural law are more difficult conclusions drawn from primary and secondary principles. Human beings may be guilty of inculpable ignorance of some of these principles because they are derived through more complicated reasoning. They are not immediately evident, and a person could be invincibly ignorant or have different interpretations of them. For example, telling a lie to save another person's life may at first appear to be ethical and moral.

Based on the foregoing three kinds of principles, it is clear that all people may not necessarily arrive at the same conclusions regarding morality, particularly as far as tertiary principles are concerned. While general principles of natural law are the same for all people, not every person will correctly deduce particular conclusions from those general principles. Aquinas correctly said: "The more we descend toward the particular, the more frequently we encounter defects."[11]

Aquinas discussed the problems of arriving at accurate knowledge of the principles of natural law as follows:

In speculative matters truth is the same in all men, both as to principles and conclusions; although the truth is not known to all as regards the conclusions, but only as regards the principles which are called common notions. But in matters of action, truth or practical rectitude is not the same for all as to what is particular, but only as to the common principles; and where there is the same rectitude in relation to particulars, it is not equally known to all.[12]

Thus, while natural law is universal, all human beings may not subscribe to its general principles in the same way. Natural law is universal in principle, but does not necessarily result in the same actions.

A second quality of natural law is its *immutability*—that is, it does not change. It remains the same for human beings of all places and at all times.

The reason natural law does not change is that human nature does not change. This means that at least its first principles do not change, though there may be changes in some secondary and tertiary principles, in that research and scientific discoveries clarify matters previously unclear. Natural law will last as long as there are human beings; it cannot be abolished from the heart.[13]

Effects of Natural Law

Natural law is not as simple or as clear as the Judge Thomas confirmation hearings suggested. In a way, human beings are still discovering some principles of natural law. There is still disagreement among people of good will as to what these principles are, particularly the tertiary principles.

Given that natural law exists, two effects follow. Natural law not only tells us what is good, it also imposes a moral obligation to do good and avoid evil. A moral obligation is the necessity of carrying out something commanded by law. We must obey. Natural law imposes a moral obligation on all human beings, regardless of race, religion or sex, to obey its principles. That is what St. Thomas Aquinas had in mind when he said that the word *law* comes from the Latin *ligare*, which means "to bind."[14] It binds all human beings to the principles of natural law as particular human beings know them. If human beings understand these principles differently because of invincible ignorance or other such factors, they are bound to obey natural law as they understand it. In practice, this means examining the object of an action, the circumstances and the purpose. This is a position on which deontologists and teleologists should be in agreement. It involves reflection or conscience, as later discussion in this chapter will show.

The second effect follows from the notion of all laws: there are penalties and sanctions attached to natural law. For obeying natural law, there are rewards; for disobeying, there are punishments.[15] Some sanctions are natural or follow naturally from the act—as, for example, a hangover often follows a bout of drunkenness. Other sanctions are positive, in that the legislator freely applies them. For example, driving under the influence of alcohol may result in suspension of the driver's license.

Philosophers do not agree on what punishments result from violations of natural law. Since the end of humankind is ultimately at stake, and natural law ultimately aims at leading us to that end, discussion of ultimate purpose follows. This links up with psychology, in examining the nature and eternity of the soul. But human reason alone in ethics is unable to determine whether eternal punishment of a mental or spiritual nature may await human beings who seriously violate natural law.

Positive Law

According to St. Thomas Aquinas, there are two kinds of positive law; divine and human. Human positive laws may be civil or canon. Here, I focus on human, positive, civil laws. A civil law is one that a legislator freely enacts and promulgates. In contrast, natural law, given the existence of human beings, came into being by necessity. However, civil laws and constitutions have their origin in natural law. St. Thomas Aquinas summarized it as follows: "Every human law has just so much of the nature of law as it is derived from the law of nature. But if at any point it departs from the law of nature, it is no longer a law but a perversion of law."[16]

It is obvious from the earlier discussion that natural law is generic and vague. It is not sufficient to eliminate human ignorance, particularly concerning its tertiary principles. Essentially, civil laws do three things: (1) they sometimes declare or repeat natural law; (2) they sometimes determine or clarify what natural law contains, particularly the tertiary principles; and (3) they often concern issues not commanded or forbidden by natural law.

Mere declaration or repetition of natural law usually causes no problems. But when civil laws attempt to clarify or make explicit principles that supposedly are implicit in natural law, problems can arise. Everyone may not agree with that clarification or interpretation. The same applies to civil laws that have nothing to do with natural law; some may see them as interfering with natural law. And this leads to the issue of obedience or obligation to obey positive laws. It further leads to the distinction between legality and morality.

OBLIGATION TO OBEY CIVIL LAWS

If positive laws are based on natural law and often clarify natural law, there is an obligation to obey positive laws. This moral obligation rests on the assumption that positive laws conform to natural law, or do not command what natural law forbids or forbid what natural law commands. This, however, is an assumption. Obeying civil laws rests on the assumption that there is a lawful government with proper authority which enacted the law, that the laws are not contrary to natural law, that the civil laws are morally possible to obey, that they are for the common good and that the lawful authority has sufficiently promulgated it.[17] If any of these conditions is absent, citizens need not obey a particular civil law. This is the argument favoring civil disobedience, however such disobedience may be illegal and result in punishment.

Civil disobedience is what Jerry Harvey (see chapter 1) had in mind when he said that it is sometimes illegal to be moral. By engaging in civil disobedience or subscribing to a higher law than a civil law, a person may indeed be acting morally but illegally. Theoretically, civil laws should emanate from natural law, and therefore legality and morality should be identical. A recent editorial in *The Tablet* summarizes the issue:

Law and morality closely interconnect but do not merge. Their functions are distinct and so are their contents. . . . The law must make room within limits for divergent convictions. It can be done only by endowing the law with flexibility at the edges and by legislators resisting the temptation to be absolute.[18]

In practice, then, legality and morality may not be the same thing. A person can act morally but break a civil law at the same time. A person can be sent to jail for violations of civil law even when she was acting morally or ethically. In this case, the law is unjust.

The pro-life movement often takes this position to show its opposition to abortion. Its proponents see abortion as contrary to natural law, in that it allows the taking of an innocent human life. Consequently, they engage in protest marches or sitins in front of abortion clinics, which may be contrary to local law. These acts of civil disobedience are a means of demonstrating the pro-life advocate's perceived unjustness of the civil law or court decision that permits abortion. The demonstrators appeal to a higher law, and in demonstrating, they risk arrest, imprisonment and monetary fines. Public administrators, particularly police, sometimes must decide to either arrest the demonstrators or ignore them.

What about the converse? Can something be legal but viewed by many as immoral? Of course it can. The U.S. Supreme Court decision *Roe v. Wade* made abortion available and legal in the United States. According to the pro-life crowd, the Supreme Court guaranteed something in civil law that is contrary to natural law. Natural law holds that murder is wrong; since pro-life people say abortion is murder, therefore those who participate in abortions are behaving in an immoral manner. This includes patients, medical personnel and others who aid and abet abortion. Some would extend involvement in abortion to anyone who promotes, encourages, counsels in favor of, pays for or even refers a client to another agency for abortion. Of course, subjectively or in conscience, nobody would subscribe to this absolutist point of view, as the discussion on conscience later in the chapter shows.

The general assumption is that civil law must be obeyed. But this assumption must be verified to show that relevant conditions pertain to the particular law. Individual citizens may see the meaning of a law differently or regard a particular law as contrary to natural law. Thus, civil disobedience is a response to higher law and sometimes invokes the law of God as the one to be obeyed. St. Thomas Aquinas labels civil laws that do not conform to natural law as "unjust" and says: "Those laws do not bind in conscience, except perhaps to avoid scandal or disturbance, for which cause a man should even yield his right."[19] The matter of conscience is discussed later in this chapter.

Duration of Positive Laws

Unlike natural law, positive, civil laws may cease in time. When a civil law ceases, it no longer binds the citizen. Laws cease in four ways: (1) when the lawmaker abrogates the law; (2) when the purpose or the circumstances of the law change or the lawmaker enacts a new law to take the place of an existing law; (3) when they are contrary to custom; and (4) when waivers or dispensations end them,[20] whereby the law remains in force, but for serious reasons it no longer binds a particular person.

Civil laws may also cease because of privilege—that is, favored persons may be exempt; for example, legislation for mandatory military service in the United States exempted members of the clergy. Finally, civil laws may partly cease to exist for a particular citizen under "epikeia." This is a conclusion drawn by a particular person that if the legislator knew of the particular circumstances confronting this individual here and now, the legislator would exempt the person from the law.[21] For example, if a person is suffering a heart attack and attempts to drive himself in this emergency situation to a hospital, the legislator would exempt the driver from stopping at red lights or stop signs. This does not mean that a police officer would view the situation in the same way, though in practice most policemen would. This is a subjective interpretation of the law, and if made by a person in all circumstances, would negate the very notion of civil law.

The principles of civil law also apply to rules and regulations; however unlike laws, individuals, organizations or groups can make rules. Rules need not be for the common good; they can be for the private good and they usually bind persons wherever they go. But rules, too, must not violate natural law. Rules or regulations should declare or clarify civil laws, just as civil laws declare or clarify natural law. Rules and regulations can be extra guidance to public administrators as to what is right and wrong. The presumption is that rule makers have not violated natural law or civil laws, but sometimes they circumvent what the civil law clearly states. While a superior can punish a subordinate for violating the rules, if the rule is contrary to civil or natural law, the violator may have acted ethically. As with laws, a person has no obligation to obey an immoral rule.

Above and Outside the Law

Is anyone above the law? Some philosophers have argued that the sovereign—the lawmaker—is above the law because there is no one competent to pass sentence on him or her.[22] St. Thomas Aquinas denies that the sovereign is above the law because the sovereign can subject himself or herself to the law. He says that "whatever law a man makes for another, he should kekep himself."[23]

A person may be outside the law if he is in a country or territory different from the legislator's. Thus, U.S. laws may not bind a U.S. citizen residing in England.[24] The principle of epikeia also applies. The purpose of the law is to serve the common good. But if, in a particular case, observance of a law would be injurious to the common good, there is no obligation to observe the law. In this case, the spirit of the law takes precedence over the letter of the law.[25]

Summation

Natural law provides some general guidance on what is right and wrong for human beings. While human reason is capable of discovering some principles of natural law, these principles are often vague and general. People can be invincibly ignorant of some principles of natural law.

Because of the vagueness of natural law, positive laws based on natural law are necessary to clarify at least some principles. Together natural law and positive laws provide guidance on the morality of human actions.

There are so many laws, rules and regulations that govern human behavior that it is virtually impossible for any human being to know all of them. Perhaps that is where the teleologist is correct in saying that we do not need standards to govern human behavior; the human intellect alone is capable of knowing and judging what is right and what is wrong. Information, reflection, judgment, decision and action are the criteria for determining morality. This approach makes sense and is a valid response to the fact that knowledge of all laws and rules is virtually impossible.

While deontologists are content with focusing on laws and rules as the principal guidance for public administrators on morality, even they recognize that laws and regulations are insufficient. Without conscience to apply those laws and rules to particular actions, public administrators are missing a critical element. The next section examines conscience as a mechanism for deciding what is right and what is wrong.

CONSCIENCE

The discussion of law focused on principles of morality outside human beings. Conscience is something within human beings that determines the morality of human actions. Conscience is a special act of the mind that comes into being when the intellect passes judgment on the goodness or badness of a particular act. It is a practical judgment on particular, concrete, human actions.

From a deontological perspective, conscience is a judgment—an act of the intellect. It is not a feeling or an emotion, but, rather, an intellectual decision. It is also a decision with a view to a particular action. Conscience can make a practical judgment on the morality of either a past action or an action about to occur.

Conscience is different from law. Law states a *general* rule concerning actions; conscience lays down a *practical* rule for specific action. Conscience applies the law or rule to specific actions, therefore it is wider than law. Some have said that conscience is to law as a brush is to paint.

From a teleological viewpoint, conscience is quite similar to completion of the ego identity discussed by McSwain and White, whereby "every ego is in some sense a code of ethics."[26] If ego and conscience are similar or identical, people have the capacity of determining the meaning of a particular action, past or present, and at the same time assess the morality of that action. Both approaches involve reflection, assessing both meaning and morality. The deontologist uses conscience to apply the law to a particular action. The teleologist may not admit application of a particular law to give meaning or morality to an action, but if McSwain and White are correct, this process involves application of "a set of value commitments" developed by all human beings from childhood. In practice, both schools use the same process but with different tools. The moral decisions *may* be different, but since both approaches involve the same human reason, moral judgments frequently will be the same.

Types of Conscience

Human beings can have different kinds of conscience. The first is a true conscience, which means that judgment is in accordance with fact. The judgment is a correct or accurate application of law to the action. A conscience is erroneous when the judgment is false—the practical judgment incorrectly applies law to the action. The erroneous judgment can be vincibly or invincibly false, and is identical with the situations discussed regarding ignorance in chapter 4.

Conscience may be certain, doubtful or probable. A conscience is certain when the judgment on the morality of an action is without prudent fear of error. Prudent fear of error does not involve metaphysical certainty, but generally any normal person has no doubts about the judgment. That certainty can apply to both a correct and an erroneous conscience.

A conscience is doubtful when the judgment does not exclude all prudent fear of error. The person is aware of some doubts about the practical judgment to be made. A conscience can be both doubtful and erroneous at the same time.

A conscience is probable when the judgment "almost" excludes all prudent fear of error. A normal person is almost certain the judgment is correct, even though it may be erroneous.

Ethical Principles Governing Conscience

The discussion of conscience leads to the following principles governing conscience:

1. A person must take reasonable care to ensure a correct conscience.
2. A person is bound to follow a certain conscience even if that conscience is false. For example, if I am certain that it is morally right to lie to save another's life, I am bound to lie.
3. It is never ethically correct to act on a doubtful conscience. Vincible ignorance does not excuse—the person must make some effort to resolve the doubt. If efforts to resolve the doubt fail, the principle *lex dubia non obligat* ("a doubtful law does not bind") comes into play.

When is a law doubtful? There are four principles that apply and the actor is at liberty to follow the principle that appeals most.

1. A law is doubtful and does not bind when there is more probable evidence on the side of liberty than against it. This is probabilism. For example, a person in doubt about what day it is observes four calendars. Three indicate it is one day and the fourth indicates that it is a different day. The person may follow the date indicated by or deduced from the three calendars if that ensures more liberty.
2. A second version of probabilism states that the person may follow an option in favor of liberty, provided the evidence in favor of liberty is *solidly*

probable, even though the evidence against liberty is more probable. In the same example, the person may follow the time indicated by the fourth calendar even though the other three numerically appear to offer more probable evidence.

3. Another version of probabilism, equiprobabilism states that the person may follow an opinion in favor of liberty if the evidence on both sides is equally balanced. In the above example, if two calendars show that it is one day and the other two indicate that it is a different day, the person may follow either option.

4. Compensationalism says that the person should consider the evidence not only favoring and opposing liberty but also the gravity of the law, the reason for acting against the law, the inconvenience arising from following the strict interpretation of the law and the justness of the cause for selecting the option offering most liberty.

Some laws may be doubtful and provide options for people. These serve as additional guidelines to the principles of conscience just discussed. But one final question on conscience remains: Is there an additional obligation for people according to their state in life or educational status to have correct consciences? Framed in public administration terminology, the question is: Are public managers or administrators bound to educate their consciences according to the responsibilities they have?

In other contexts, management involves getting things done with the help of other people.[27] That assumes that management means getting things done *right*. Here, the argument is that getting things done right is only one side of the coin. Management also involves getting the *right* thing done. What is the right thing? What is the ethical thing to do?

If public managers must not only do things right but also do what is right, they have an obligation to educate their consciences according to their state in life. This includes not only management theory and practice but also ethical theory and practice. If managers do not do both, they run the risk of not only being outdated but also of neglecting true managerial responsibility. If managers are educators and teachers, surely they must learn both aspects of the job if they are to fulfill their role of teaching and coaching others.[28]

In educating and updating the conscience, there are two extremes to be avoided. One is not caring about conscience at all—making no effort to learn what is right or what is wrong, or perhaps showing no interest in right and wrong. Some public managers exhibit this characteristic. The other extreme is the person unable to distinguish serious actions from those that are not, whether getting things done right or doing the right thing. There are some public managers who fit this description. Neither extreme is in accord with the concept of conscience, which involves a practical judgment on the morality of human action.

CONCLUSION

This chapter examined laws, rules and conscience as sources of ethical guidance. Besides reliance on the nature of an action, its consequences and purpose, laws, rules and conscience provide guidance in determining what is right and what is wrong. However, in spite of the help that laws, rules and conscience may be to a public administrator, they do not guarantee infallible judgment. While laws and rules would seem to be a deontologically sound frame of reference in making ethical decisions, there are many flaws. The teleological approach acknowledges that there are too many civil laws, rules, regulations, court decisions and opinions governing almost everything, including ethical decisions. It is virtually impossible for a public administrator to know all the laws or rules. However, the discussion attempted to provide a framework for understanding civil laws, rules, regulations by linking them with natural law and human reason. The discussion on conscience attempted further to expand this framework and provide a basis for ethical decision making. The end result is far from perfect, but at least a starting point.

From a teleological perspective, if conscience and ego are similar or the same, there are flaws resulting from the interpretations or decisions of what is right and what is wrong. There is no doubt that reflection on the meaning of an action is an important factor in determining its morality. Rather than the public administrator attempting to understand all the laws, rules, regulations, court decisions and opinions, the teleological approach may be the one to apply in discretionary decision making. This may not always satisfy top management, but it is not without solid philosophical support and, indeed, practical merit. But regardless of whether public administrators follow a deontological or a teleological approach, thinking, reasoning and reflection must occur. Otherwise, there is no way to hold public administrators accountable for their actions.

In considering what is right and wrong, public administrators have at their disposal information on the nature of the action performed or about to be performed, the circumstances surrounding the action and the purpose of the action. In addition, laws, rules and regulations provide additional guidance. Everyone has a conscience that can apply those laws, rules and other criteria of morality to specific actions. Except for what religion and theology have to offer, and they have much, that is all public administrators have to make discretionary administrative decisions. Ethics may indeed shortchange them. But if it does, it shortchanges people in all walks of life. The foregoing is the best that human reason can offer as a theoretical framework for assessing morality.

This concludes the discussion on general ethics. The task in special ethics is to attempt to apply these general and sometimes vague principles to special situations, particularly to situations that confront public administrators. What is right for individuals is largely determined by the rights of those individuals and the duties those people are bound to perform. The next chapter addresses human rights and duties, and in particular people's duties to themselves.

NOTES

1. Anton C. Pegis, ed., *Basic Writings of St. Thomas Aquinas*, Volume Two (New York: Random House, 1945), p. 747.

2. Ibid., p. 743.

3. Ibid., pp. 744–47.

4. Ibid., p. 796.

5. Judgment delivered on the 5th day of March 1992 by C. J. Finlay in *The Attorney General v. X and Others*, The Supreme Court of Ireland 47/92.

6. Pegis, *Basic Writings of St. Thomas Aquinas*, pp. 748ff.

7. Ibid., pp. 750–93.

8. Ibid., p. 750.

9. Paul John Bradley, ed., *The Holy Bible* (Catholic Action Edition). Gustonia, N.C.: Goodwill Publishers, 1953, p. 180.

10. Pegis, *Basic Writings of St. Thomas Aquinas*, pp. 774–75.

11. Ibid., p. 777.

12. Ibid., p. 777.

13. Ibid., pp. 780–81.

14. Ibid., p. 743.

15. Ibid., pp. 760–61.

16. Ibid., p. 784.

17. Ibid., pp. 787–88, 793–97.

18. *The Tablet* 246, no. 7910 (March 14, 1992), p. 331.

19. Pegis, *Basic Writings of St. Thomas Aquinas*, pp. 792–95.

20. Ibid., p. 792.

21. Ibid., p. 798. See also T. Lincoln Bouscaren and Adam C. Ellis, *Canon Law: A Text and Commentary*, p. 33. Milwaukee: Bruce, 1951.

22. Ibid., pp. 796–97.

23. Ibid., p. 797.

24. Ibid., p. 796.

25. Ibid., p. 798.

26. Cynthia J. McSwain and Orion F. White, "The Case for Lying, Cheating and Stealing—Personal Development as Ethical Guidance for Managers," *Administration and Society, 18*, no. 4 (February 1987), p. 419.

27. Patrick J. Sheeran, "Managers are Learners and Teachers," in *How Public Organizations Work: Learning from Experience*, Christopher Bellavita, ed. (New York: Praeger, 1990), p. 21.

28. Ibid., p. 27.

PART II

Special Ethics

CHAPTER 7

Human Rights and Duties—Duties to Ourselves

Part I defined *ethics*, examined what constitutes a human action, and developed certain principles to determine whether human actions are good, bad or indifferent. Special ethics applies these principles to concrete situations. In applying these principles to situations, it is important to understand that the rights a particular person possesses and the duties he or she is bound to perform often determine what is right and wrong for that person. For example, it is one thing to observe a man strike another without provocation, but it is quite a different matter to see the stricken man strike back. The latter action may be one of self-defense, and therefore moral in reaction to the first situation. So in applying the principles of ethics to specific situations, it is useful to do so in terms of rights and duties. But first we should consider the notion of rights and duties in general. The second half of this chapter focuses on some of our duties toward ourselves. Later chapters examine duties toward other human beings, and rights and duties as members of society and the state.

HUMAN RIGHTS

Human rights became a major theme in the Carter administration. They continue to be a major topic of discussion, not only in the United States but also internationally. The issue of animal rights has also become an important topic, particularly in the United States. A right is a moral, just, legal, and inviolable power or claim of a person over something which is his or her own. It is equivalent to ownership. While a right may involve a claim to something physical, that claim does not extend to other human beings. However, a person may have the right to services from other human beings. A right involves four things:

1. The subject of a right is the being who possesses a right. An individual person or a group of people may possess rights. (The issues of animal rights is a matter for others to discuss.)
2. The object of a right is the matter over which a person exercises the right.
3. The title of a right is the foundation or the origin of the right. It is that which establishes the right, such as a constitution or a law.
4. The term of a right is the person or persons who have the corresponding duty to observe a right.

Kinds of Human Rights

Some rights are natural, in that natural law confers or establishes them. Other rights are positive, in that positive laws confer them. Some rights are connatural because human beings possess them from birth and they are independent of laws. Acquired rights are those conferred on us by others, such as constitutions or laws. Some rights are public, such as the state's right to govern, whereas other rights are private because groups or persons possess them. In practice, private rights refer to an organization's capacity to make rules.

The most important sets of rights are the inalienable and alienable. Inalienable rights are those that we cannot renounce, such as the right to life. Alienable rights are those that can be renounced, given up or transferred. If smoking is a right, it is obvious that it is an alienable right that the smoker can give up. Likewise, the right to marry is an alienable right, or one which a person can voluntarily forgo.

Qualities of Rights

All human rights have three qualities: coercion, limitation and collision. *Coercion* means that the possessor of a right has the power or capacity to use physical force to protect a right or to remove obstacles to exercising that right. Coercion means that we can use physical force to defend a human right, or we can inflict a penalty to restore a violated right. The right remains in force even though the possessor of the right is unable to exercise the right.

Who possesses the power of coercion? The possessor of the right and the person in authority who represents the possessor of the right—the state. The notion of coercion provides the state with the authority to defend and vindicate its sovereign rights against unjust aggression. A war may be a just means to protect or recover rights, for instance. More will be said later in the chapter on the notion of what constitutes a just war.

The second quality of rights is *limitation*. Limitation means all human rights are limited, by reason that all human rights come from natural law, which does not confer absolute rights on everybody. Human rights are limited because the exercise of one right is curtailed by exercise of another right. Some people illustrate this point as: "Your right to swing your arm stops at my nose!"

The purpose for which rights are granted limits the exercise of those rights. All human beings have the same ultimate end and the same right to pursue that end. Consequently, the rights of others limit the exercise of our rights. Duty also limits the exercise of rights. I may have a right to drive a car (although some states call this a privilege), but I have a corresponding duty not to kill others while driving. Consequently, if I have a right to drive, my duty to be careful limits my right.

The third characteristic of rights is *collision*. Collision means that there may be apparent conflicts among rights. Since all rights ultimately originate from natural law, there can be no real conflict between rights. But our ability to resolve apparent conflicts between rights is imperfect. We are often unable to determine the gradations among rights. Three principles help to resolve apparent conflicts between rights:

1. Rights originating from higher law or those that are more necessary for the common good should prevail. Natural rights prevail over positive rights.
2. The superiority of the person involved usually carries with it the superiority of that person's rights. The rights of self prevail over the rights of others. The rights of relatives usually have preference over the rights of friends.
3. Rights that concern noble or universal causes prevail over rights pertaining to things of less value. Therefore, the rights of the soul or the mind prevail over the rights of the body.

The U.S. Constitution guarantees some fundamental rights, but does not enumerate all the rights Americans have. The U.S. Supreme Court is the custodian and interpreter of the Constitution. Some citizens, and especially some politicians, have accused the Supreme Court of finding "new" rights in the Constitution not intended by the framers. They claim that one of those is the right of a woman to have an abortion.

Some scholars think that Americans have no rights other than those guaranteed by the Constitution. To them, "natural rights" refers only to the fundamental rights actually guaranteed by the Constitution.[1] During the U.S. Senate confirmation hearings for proposed Supreme Court Justice Clarence Thomas, there was considerable debate on this issue, particularly whether the Court should examine natural law when discussing issues not clearly contained in the U.S. Constitution. The previous chapter addressed the difficulties involved in interpreting natural law, and these same difficulties pertain to the precise human rights natural law confirms.

The United Nations has a Commission on Human Rights. The following is a partial list of those rights on which many nations agree. The agreement does not necessarily mean, however, that all member nations have a good record in observing these human rights.

1. The right to life and bodily integrity
2. The right to worship in private and in public
3. The right to a religious formation through education and formation
4. The right to personal liberty under just laws
5. The right to equal protection under just laws regardless of sex, nationality, color or creed
6. The right to freedom of expression, information and communication according to truth and justice
7. The right to choose and maintain a state of life
8. The right to a suitable education for the development and maintenance of a person's dignity as a human person
9. The right to petition a government to redress grievances
10. The right to a nationality
11. The right of access to the means of livelihood by migration
12. The right of association and peaceable assembly
13. The right to work and choose an occupation
14. The right to a living wage (and perhaps a just wage)
15. The right to personal ownership, use and disposal of property subject to the rights of others and limitations in the interests of the general welfare
16. The right to collective bargaining
17. The right to associate by industries and professions to obtain economic justice
18. The right to assistance from society and if necessary from the state in distress of person or family

In addition to individual rights, the following is a partial list of family rights:

1. The right to marry, establish a home and beget children
2. The right to economic security sufficient for independence of the family
3. The right to the protection of maternity
4. The right to educate children
5. The right to maintain by public protection and assistance if necessary adequate standards of child welfare within the family
6. The right to assistance through community service in the education and care of children
7. The right to housing conducive to means and functions of family life
8. The right of immunity of the home from search and trespass
9. The right of protection against immoral conditions in the community

DUTIES

While human beings have limited natural rights, they also have corresponding duties stemming from those rights. *Duty* is often defined as a moral obligation to do something or omit something. There is a binding of the will to perform or not perform. But a duty is not exactly the same as an obligation, which really refers to a superior. A superior imposes an obligation, whereas a duty binds a person to do or omit something in favor of somebody else, whether a superior, an equal or a subordinate.

Human beings are not only rational, they are also social. They have duties to the Supreme Being, to themselves and other human beings. Theodicy discusses our duties to the Supreme Being. In the remainder of this chapter, I confine the discussion of our duty to ourselves. The next chapter examines our duty to other human beings.

Our Duty to Ourselves

We have no duty in justice to ourselves. However, we are bound to love ourselves in an ordinate or reasonable manner. This sometimes is summed up as follows: You should be first your own best friend. This is not a bad way for a public administrator to begin. How can you think well of or treat other people fairly and decently if you hate yourself or have a poor self-image? Chapter 3 showed that people are composed of a body and a soul. We therefore have two sets of duties—one to our soul and the other to our body.

Duty to the Soul (Intellect)

The first duty to our soul or intellect is to educate our faculties to gain at least an elementary knowledge of whether there is a Supreme Being. This duty also includes knowledge sufficient to help us carry out the duties of our particular state in life. For public administrators, that means taking the necessary course either through formal training, on-the-job training or both to meet the responsibilities of the job. Furthermore, duty to the intellect includes training the will in decision making so that our decisions are morally good. Management not only involves teaching others to do things right, it also involves teaching them to do the right thing.[2]

Care of the Body

Our duty to our body has two aspects: negative and positive. Under negative duties, we are bound not to kill ourselves. Suicide is the *direct* killing of oneself on one's own authority. Indirect killing results from some action directly intended for another effect, but from which death may be foreseen but is not intended. A hunger strike is an example of indirect killing because the primary intention in abstaining from food and drink may involve a freedom, but while death may be foreseen as a result, it is not intended.

Most ethicists claim that suicide is contrary to natural law because humans, together with all animals, have imbedded in their nature an instinct for self-preservation. Suicide is contrary to that instinct. In addition, we belong to society, the family and the state. We owe these institutions something for the benefits they have conferred on us. With suicide, we deprive society of its claims on us. We fail to fulfill our duty to society.

Others such as Joseph Fletcher claim that suicide, particularly euthanasia, may be moral. Fletcher makes no distinction between negative efforts that result in the occurrence of death and positive efforts in which a person does something deliberate to hasten death. It is a teleological approach and the end—the consequences of the action—is the only element that need be considered.[3]

Mutilation means depriving oneself of one's faculties or bodily organs. Is mutilation of the body contrary to natural law? Is it morally right to perform surgery to remove a diseased bodily member? Here we enter the realm of medical ethics; clearly, many issues in medical ethics affect public policy and public administration.

Obviously, when surgery is needed to preserve life or health, the surgical procedure is not contrary to natural law and, in fact, is moral. Surgery in such cases appears to be ordinary care which will be addressed later in this chapter. However, some people would deny that surgery in any circumstance is ordinary care. But what about voluntary surgical procedures done for eugenic purposes? What about removal of an appendix that is not diseased because a person is about to visit a country where there are few physicians and where access to medicine will be difficult? What about voluntary sterilization? Do we own our own bodies and can we do with them as we please?

These are tough questions. We have certain inalienable rights, which we cannot give up. The right to life is one of these. We have a corresonding duty to maintain that life and to maintain the human body to the best of our ability. Some ethicists claim that ordinary care of the human body prohibits voluntary mutilations such as voluntary sterilization, usually performed to render conception impossible. This is an issue that often confronts physicians, clinics and hospitals. It is one that affects some public administrators, particularly in the health and human services area, who establish regulations and provide funding for these kinds of procedures. Are these procedures ethical? Jonsen and Hellegers write: "Because ultimately he is not his own man, man has an obligation to preserve his life and health. Any mutilation of the body is an abuse of the divine dominion, unless that mutilation contributes to the good of the whole body."[4] This view is based on the principle of totality—that is, "the integrity of the physical organism of an individual person."[5] The view is deeply rooted in the theory that all bodily members are parts of human nature. The theory is that we do not own our bodies; we may only use them. Consequently, there must be just cause, such as preservation of life or health, to interfere with or mutilate a bodily organ. To do otherwise would be considered immoral.

Another school of thought is that we have control over our bodies. The claim "Our bodies are our own" summarizes this philosophy, and its proponents maintain that medical procedures such as voluntary sterilization, are not morally life-threatening and can be performed at will. Others require a "just cause" or reason for such a procedure. What would constitute such a just reason? The decision is a matter of conscience—a subjective decision as to whether sterilization is moral.

People who follow the teleological theory consider the particular surgical procedure, the merits of the case and decide accordingly; there are no objective rules involved. However, they may come to the same decision as those who have a deontological perspective. Some subscribers to deontological theory look for a just cause or a just reason for performing voluntary sterilization. The latter may argue that, to perform a procedure of this kind as a means of permanent birth control, either for convenience or because other methods do not work, certainly is a cause that appears reasonable. An appropriate cause is needed to offset compliance with our duty to preserve our bodily integrity, or the principle of totality. Some argue that convenience or the unsuitability of other family planning methods does not constitute just cause. In other words, they feel a good end does not justify a bad means.

Some ethicists maintain that eugenic sterilizations performed by the state to prevent conception of children by undesirable persons, such as the physically or mentally handicapped, are ethical. While the state has the right to enforce laws and punish offenders and may have the power to exercise capital punishment, as is discussed in chapter 10, it is felt that every human being has a right to his or her bodily integrity, and eugenic sterilizations for undesirable persons violate a person's rights. The U.S. Department of Health and Human Services has issued specific regulations that prohibit such practices.

While the rights of the physically and mentally handicapped to bodily integrity appear clear, it is not so clear whether the state has the power to punish by sterilizing criminals habitually guilty of sexual crimes, such as rape or child sex abuse. If the state has the right and the authority to inflict capital punishment for certain types of murder, it also has the right to inflict sterilization on these habitual criminals. This power is the state's right to act for the common good. (I address the issue of capital punishment later; what applies to capital punishment also applies to eugenic sterilization.)

The arguments opposing sterilization center on the object of the action—the surgical procedure—the circumstances and the purpose of the action. Some maintain that the surgical procedure is, by its very nature, evil and therefore the circumstances or purpose can never make this procedure moral. It is difficult to adhere to this view, since obviously the procedure is not immoral when done for medical or health reasons. It is not an intrinsically evil act; it may even be an indifferent act in itself. Instead, the circumstances and purpose may ultimately determine the morality of voluntary sterilization. And both may vary in individual circumstances so that the same action can either be moral or immoral. That is another reason why some deontologists require the existence of a reasonable cause for such surgical procedures.

This issue is a clear example of the difference between legality and morality. Family planning is legal in the United States and voluntary sterilization is a legal method of family planning. Some theorists argue that most methods of family planning are immoral because they frustrate certain principles of natural law. Could it be that federal law is contrary to natural law in this instance? The presumption is that positive law and natural law are in agreement. In addition, government has regulations to safeguard against involuntary sterilization and ensure informed consent. These regulations render the procedure legal. Yet for some, the positive law is contrary to natural law. For them, the higher law must be obeyed; if not, there is a violation of the principle of totality.

One of the purposes of family planning is to enable couples to space their children, thus to provide adequately for them. Voluntary sterilization is a sure method of preventing unwanted pregnancies and provides some assurance that children already born will be provided for. For many, that is a sufficiently just reason to undergo voluntary sterilization.

If we look on voluntary sterilization as having two effects—the good effect is prevention of future unwanted pregnancies and enhancement of the marriage, and the bad effect is the severing of a bodily member—we could strongly argue that the good effect takes precedence as long as it is the primary intended effect.

But some argue that sterilization is against natural law for another reason. They see the primary end of sex in marriage only as procreation. Marriage, they argue, is a natural state evolving from natural law. This assertion may involve a connection that human reason is not quite capable of deducing. They claim that voluntary sterilization interferes with the process of procreation and therefore is an intrinsically evil act.

The example of sterilization affects many professionals in both the public and private sectors. For instance, it involves public administrators who distribute or receive public funds for family planning programs. Are these administrators acting ethically when they distribute these funds for purposes that they view as unethical? Are they just "carrying out the law"? Is carrying out the law sufficient reason for them to justify what they consider unethical conduct? Public servants who administer these programs or distribute these funds may have few options, including seeking a job with another institution that does not promote family planning. Perhaps a riskier approach is to try to have the law they regard as unethical changed.

Chapter 1 stressed that ethics will not resolve all human problems. Chapter 3 pointed out the flaws in human reasoning. Ethics does not present prepackaged, agreed-on principles or solutions to the morality of human actions. But people have a conscience, and in the last resort that conscience must decide what is right or moral for them in a particular case.

Ordinary vs. Extraordinary Means

How much care is a human being bound to devote to preserving his or her own health and bodily integrity? Ethicists generally agree that human beings are bound to take ordinary means to preserve health. All do not agree on what constitutes ordinary means. Briefly, ordinary means includes proper food, diet, and exercise. Does it involve having health insurance, making regular visits to a physician or avoiding alcohol, smoking, drugs? Does it mean no sex or just "safe sex"? Some argue that all these are minimum ordinary means. Others argue that some of these are extraordinary means.

Extraordinary means may include having the best possible health insurance, the most comprehensive exercise program, the best physician, access to the best medical procedures. Are heart and kidney transplants extraordinary procedures? Many years ago they certainly were, but today they are more common. Yet a person is not bound to go to extremes to preserve health and bodily integrity.

Medical ethics discusses these issues more thoroughly. But there are other thorny problems in this area that policy makers at all levels of government must confront. Issues such as in vitro fertilization, for instance, raise questions of ethics. Are in vitro fertilizations ethical? Again, there are two schools of thought, one saying they are and the other saying they are not. Is it ethical for a woman to have her husband's sperm injected into her so as to make conception more likely? Some people have questioned the method by which the sperm are collected; the method of collection determines the morality of in vitro fertilization. Other people see no ethical problem with in vitro fertilization as long as the husband's sperm are used.

But what about when the donor is someone other than the husband? Some people see no ethical problem; others view it as an immoral act—the end (pregnancy) does not justify the means. Human reason as used in ethics is not able to go beyond this point through deductive reasoning to provide a universally acceptable answer.

Other ethical problems arise from the use of fetal tissue in medical research. The U.S. government policy is not to fund research on fetal tissue procured through induced abortion; if the fetal tissue comes from spontaneous miscarriages or ectopic pregnancies, that is a different matter. Yet private researchers do both and consider them ethical. Their argument is that, regardless of how the tissue is obtained, research on that tissue is ethical. The tissue is used in research to treat illnesses such as diabetes and Parkinson's disease.

But there is a potential problem in the use of fetal tissue obtained through an abortion if a woman who got pregnant intended to have the abortion to provide such tissue. Most ethicists argue that such tissue should be used, but question the morality of having an abortion for such purposes.

In regard to extraordinary means, one might ask what precautions, if any, should test pilots, daredevils, circus performers and many athletes take to ensure health and bodily integrity? Clearly, ethics does not forbid participation in these events, but following the principle of ordinary means, these persons should be skilled, trained, physically fit, knowledgeable, cautious and alert. Beyohnd that, it is difficult to determine where extraordinary means begin or what constitutes extraordinary means in every situation.

Reputation and Self-Support

Every human being has, by nature, a duty to obtain and maintain a good name among his or her fellow beings. Many civil laws enforce this principle to the extent of not requiring a person to incriminate himself or herself in judicial matters. In fact, a good reputation is as important to a person as life itself, and may be defended in the same way. The five principles governing self-defense (see section following) also apply in defending a good name. And as chapter 10 discusses, they equally apply to a nation's right to defend and protect its citizens even by war—a just war.

Likewise, people have a duty to acquire as many earthly possessions as necessary to support themselves and their family, provided they have the ability and opportunity to work. Chapter 9 addresses this issue more fully.

THE RIGHT TO SELF-DEFENSE

The right to self-defense brings with it a corresponding duty to protect our lives and bodily integrity against an unjust aggressor. This is an instinctive right arising from natural law. Thomas Hobbes focused almost solely on this right and its corresponding duty.[6]

What is an unjust aggressor? This is a human being who either directly attacks or is just about to attack another person, to deprive that other person of his or her life, bodily integrity or private property. The attack must be in progress or just about to happen. The action must be unjust—that is, the person attacking or about to attack has no right to attack or to invade another's right.

What does the right of self-defense entail? Human reason tells us that we can defend ourselves against unjust aggression, even to the extent of killing the aggressor. But the same human reason also tells us that we must exercise moderation in such defense. That is, while it may be moral to kill an unjust aggressor, if a less extreme action such as wounding the aggressor is possible, we should not go beyond the lesser action.

There are a few reasonable principles that arise from this conclusion.

1. The attack must be actual or proximate.
2. The attack must be unjust.
3. The attack must cause or be about to cause real danger, such as loss of life, limb or property.
4. The danger can be avoided only by self-defense—that is, by fighting back. If the victim can depart the scene, then other actions of self-defense are unnecessary and should not be taken.
5. The intention of the victim must be self-defense and not revenge.

The latter two principles ensure that the victim will not take greater means than necessary to repel the aggressor.

These principles are derived from the collision of rights principle described earlier in the chapter. In unjust aggression there is a collision of rights—a collision between the rights of the victim and the rights of the aggressor. The rights of the victim prevail because the aggressor has the option of abandoning the attack, or the person under attack is in real danger of losing life or something as important as life, such as limbs or property. It is natural, even instinctive, to prefer one's own life to that of another, as Hobbes has rightfully pointed out. Of course, claiming self-defense requires a practical judgment that may indeed be subjective, or perhaps erroneous.

NOTES

1. Robert T. Kimbrough, *Summary of American Law* (San Francisco: Bancroft-Whitney, 1974), p. 49.

2. Patrick J. Sheeran, "Managers are Learners and Teachers," in *How Public Organizations Work: Learning from Experience*, Christopher Bellavita, ed. (New York: Praeger, 1990), pp. 17–27.

3. Joseph Fletcher, "Ethics and Euthanasia," in *Morality in the Modern World*, Lawrence Habermehl, ed. (Encino, Calif.: Dickenson Publishing Company, 1976), pp. 253–56.

4. Albert R. Jonsen and Andre E. Hellegers, "Conceptual Foundations for an Ethics of Medical Care," in *Ethics for Health Care*, Laurence R. Tancredi, ed. (Washington, D.C.: National Academy of Sciences, 1974), p. 11.

5. Ibid., p. 11.

6. Thomas Hobbes, *The Leviathan*, Michael Oakeshott, ed. (New York: Macmillan, 1962).

CHAPTER 8

Duties to Other Human Beings

Our most important duties to our fellow human beings are twofold: to their minds and their bodies. To their minds, our primary duty is to speak the truth and not deliberately lead them toward evil, especially by bad example. To their bodies, our primary duty is to respect their right to life and bodily integrity. This chapter examines the philosophical roots and the principles derived from these roots that affect our ethical human relations.

LYING

To understand lying, we must first determine what is truth. Truth is conformity of speech and thought. Speech involves words, signs, writing and any means of communication. Truth, then, is conformity of what we think and what we communicate.

A lie is the opposite of truth. There is no conformity of thought and communication. Indeed, there is a contradiction between what we think and what we communicate. If a person is unaware of this contradiction, it is a material lie or simply an error. But if the communicator is aware of the contradiction and deliberately proceeds to communicate the falsehood anyway, this is a formal lie. Ethics is concerned only with formal lies. A formal lie is a conscious and deliberate statement contrary to what is in the communicator's mind.

The foregoing definition of a formal lie considers four elements: (1) There is a statement contradicting thought; (2) There is an act of the will (the decision) to state or communicate something contrary to the thought;

(3) There is at least implicit the will to deceive another person; (4) There is actual deception of another person. Most ethicists claim that the first two elements constitute the essence of a lie. All agree that the fourth element (actual deception of another person, which sometimes happens as a result of a lie) is a consequence of a lie and not the essence. But there is strong disagreement as to whether the will to deceive another is necessary to the essence of a lie. Either view is correct.

A person can lie in four different ways: (1) by affirming what he or she knows as untrue; (2) by denying what he or she knows is true; (3) by asserting as certain what he or she knows to be doubtful; (4) by asserting as doubtful what he or she knows to be certain.

According to St. Thomas Aquinas, there are three kinds of formal lies: pernicious or mischievious lies—that is, untruths told to harm another person; officious lies, or untruths told to gain an advantage for onself or another; and jocose lies, or untruths told in jest or for fun.[1]

The Morality of Lying

Some philosophers have maintained that certain kinds of lies are not morally wrong. They claim that jocose lies are not really lies—they are told in fun and often are recognized for what they are. The same applies to officious lies—the audience can often recognize them as false statements. Others maintain that a lie occurs only when a person tells an untruth to another who has a right to know the truth. But these added dimensions do not concur with the definition of a formal lie given above.

The majority of ethicists, however, state that every formal lie—whether pernicious, officious or jocose—is intrinsically evil. The argument is that natural law forbids that which is contrary to the natural purpose of speech. The natural purpose of speech is to convey one's thoughts or judgments to others. A formal lie distorts this process and is therefore contrary to natural law. It will always be a contradiction between what the mind knows and what the communication is. Hence, every lie by nature of its object is intrinsically evil, and no circumstances or purpose can change that nature to make the object good. It is true that the circumstances for which a lie was told or the purpose (such as to save another's life) may be good, but these elements make the action of lying only less bad, never good. The end does not justify the means. The teleologist, however, would dispute this view, and claim that only the circumstances and perhaps the end or purpose of the act should be considered in assessing whether telling a lie is moral or immoral. Consequently, every specific action involving an untruth must be considered, reflected on and judged to determine its morality.

A second argument supporting the claim that all formal lies are intrinsically evil is as follows. Natural law forbids that which would cause serious detriment to society. Formal lies can cause such detriments. The functions of society depend, to a large extent, on communication of ideas. Unless that communication is in accordance with our thoughts and judgments, we are not communicating our true ideas to one another. We are deceiving others and causing distrust and fraud to emerge. Hence, lying is contrary to natural law.

These teleological and deontological approaches provide public administrators with the philosophical rationale and some rules—or at least some options—in dealing with the issue of lying. Sissela Bok's excellent treatment of the practical aspects associated with lying elaborates on this topic.[2]

It is clear that society does not respect lying, and lying by persons in public office or in the public eye often results in anger, as illustrated in the Watergate and Iran-Contra affairs. Public servants should be the pillars of society. The public deeply resents any deception or even any appearance of deception on the part of its public servants. It behooves public managers to be truthful, not only because they have taken an oath of office but also to ensure their own growth and development within the public service.

Public administrators often find themselves in situations where they engage in deceptive activities or come very close to such deception. In bureaucracies in particular, there is great concern about secrecy and security. The public and other government agencies often request information. Sometimes public administrators do not provide it, and in doing so claim they do not have it when actually they do. Frequently, the information provided is a distortion of the truth. Bureaucracies spend considerable time writing, rewriting and editing materials so that the finished product is too vague to convey true meaning. Even when the person or agency requesting the information has the right to know and the information is not classified, in some cases public administrators are not as forthcoming as they should be. There is no question they sometimes distort the truth or lie.

Public agencies also apply a "spin" to their information. That is, policy makers and political personnel often want to make their programs appear in the best light, so they often portray them as very effective. They use favorable statistics or wrongly interpret the data to demonstrate what they want to show. And sometimes they omit significant details.

Some people argue that this is common practice, that it is the "done thing." Everybody does it and therefore it is not lying. But this is a matter of opinion and, at least in some cases, there is no question that the "spinners" intend deception and are therefore behaving unethically. One might ask, Why are so many public administrators and public officials afraid of the truth? Is it that they are afraid of losing their jobs or are they shamed by a poorly administered or ineffective program? Whatever the reason, these administrative practices certainly border on and often result in deception.

The area of research also often leads to and borders on deception. Sometimes researchers make bad results look good, either by deliberately skewing data or misinterpreting the findings. Again, nobody wants to look bad or be accused of incompetence. But using deceptive tactics to protect oneself is not professional behavior.

Worse still are evaluators and consultants who are awarded contracts to come up with foregone conclusions. Their approach is, "What do you want my final report to say?" Clearly, this behavior is unethical.

Mental Reservations

Sissela Bok discusses mental reservations in her book.[3] This issue arises from the focus on lying as an intrinsically evil act. If lying is intrinsically evil, all human beings have an obligation to tell the truth. But must we always divulge the whole truth? What about a corresponding duty we may have to keep a secret? By keeping silent or by answering a question, we may be directly or indirectly revealing a secret we have a duty to keep. For example, suppose a friend tells you that he stole $500 from the place where he works. The owner of the business is also your friend and asks you directly if the other friend has told you he has stolen the money. What are you to do? What is the solution to this dilemma? There are three philosophical responses:

1. Some say that it would be all right to tell an officious lie. But if every lie, including an officious lie, is intrinsically evil, an officious lie in this situation is unethical.
2. Others claim that the use of a purely mental reservation is ethically allowable in these circumstances. A purely mental reservation is really nothing short of a play on words. It does not reveal the speaker's mind, either by speech or circumstances—for example, if you said "He said he did not steal anything from you" while thinking "with his left hand." The latter provides the listener with no clue as to what is truly in your mind. Thus, most ethicists claim that a purely mental reservation is the same as a formal lie and as such is intrinsically evil.

3. Some others say that it is ethical for you to use a *broad* mental reservation. A broad mental reservation is the annunciation of a proposition containing two judgments, one of which conforms to what is in your mind and the other which does not.

A broad mental reservation is a statement that limits the full meaning of what the speaker says and provides the listener with some external indication of the limitation either from customary use, circumstances or the manner of speech. For example, if a person calls the office of another person and the receptionist says "she is not in," through customary use that statement has two meanings: the person may in fact not be in the office or she may be in the office but is "not in" to the caller. It is left to the caller to determine which is the correct meaning. It is likely that the caller will deceive himself, although he may also deduce the correct meaning from the statement. The statement containing the broad mental reservation is ambiguous or has two meanings, one of which is correct and the other is not. The listener can, from the form of the words, circumstances or manner of speech, deduce the correct meaning. Thus, the statement in a broad mental reservation is in itself true, but not the whole truth.

The broad mental reservation may seem like splitting hairs or rationalization for lying. But in fact the broad mental reservation meets all three criteria of morality. The object of the action—telling the truth—is good. The circumstances make its use necessary. The purpose can be good. In fact, a person may ethically swear under oath while using a broad mental reservation.

Ethicists, however, have developed principles that serve as guidelines for using broad mental reservations:

1. A broad mental reservation is not a formal lie because the words used do contain the truth.
2. Because the listener can attach the wrong meaning to a broad mental reservation, a good or just reason is necessary before resorting to it.
3. If the listener has a right to the truth, the speaker may not use a broad mental reservation. But who has a right to the truth? Generally people in authority, such as public officials, parents and superiors.
4. The speaker may have a duty to use a broad mental reservation when it would be unethical to reveal the whole truth and when the speaker is unable to avoid an answer. In this case, the broad mental reservation is not a formal lie and at the same time it is not the full truth. It balances a clash of two apparently conflicting duties.

Secrets

Secrets involve the question of confidentiality. Sisela Bok has provided an excellent treatment of this issue.[4] Secrets are a matter of great concern to most professionals, including public administrators. By the very nature of their work, public administrators frequently must grapple with the ethics of keeping secrets and preserving confidentiality, while at the same time being mindful of their truthfulness to society. Therefore, it is important to examine secrets and to focus on the philosophical underpinnings that provide a rationale for maintaining confidentiality.

A secret is a truth known to a person who has the right or duty not to reveal it to another person. A person has the right or duty to not reveal a secret when the truth is so connected to one's own or another's welfare that revelation of that truth would cause harm to oneself, another person, a group or the community.

There are different kinds of secrets, with escalating degrees of obligation:

1. Natural secrets are known truths which, by their very nature, require those who know them to keep them secret. For example, finding out by accident and revealing to the press a police plan to conduct a drug bust would be unethical. The very nature of the plan should inform the person who discovers it that he should not reveal it. We would need a good reason to reveal this kind of secret.

2. Promised secrets are truths not yet public that we have promised others we will not reveal. If a person requires us to promise not to reveal something before telling us the secret, and we so promise, obviously we need a just or reasonable cause to violate that promise. Otherwise, we have the duty not to reveal a promised secret.

3. Committed secrets are secrets communicated to us on the condition that we do not reveal them. Besides not being yet publicly known, they are different from promised secrets in that they have not been as yet revealed to a third party without obligation of concealment, and the revelation of the truth would result in loss or injury to the person(s) involved. All professional secrets are committed secrets. These include doctor-patient, attorney-client and counselor-client relationships as well as secrets between the clergy and their clients.

Maintaining confidentiality often presents a dilemma to public administrators. When coupled with the right to know, the issue becomes even more difficult. But it is obvious that every human being has a right to self-protection, to a positive reputation, to preservation of their life and good name of family members, relatives, friends, society and state, in that order. The same model that applies to rights also applies to duties. But does the common good sometimes prevail? In cases of child sex abuse, civil laws generally mandate professionals to reveal the names of perpetrators. The rationale is that the rights and well-being of the victim take precedence over the rights of the alleged perpetrator. Revelation of this kind of secret is for the common good, as opposed to for individual good. And so the assumption is that the civil law in this instance is not contrary to but a clarification of natural law.

THE MORALITY OF HOMICIDE

Murder is the deliberate, direct and intentional killing of another human being on the bases of one's own authority. Killing in itself is an indifferent act—as, for example, killing to defend oneself or killing a person by accident. But murder is different from manslaughter, which is the indirect killing of another person. Manslaughter involves accidental killing of another human being; however, it may be indirectly voluntary to the extent that the person foresaw the consequences of the action. Murder, on the other hand, may occur as a result of either positive actions, when a person does something that results in murder, or of negative actions, when a person withholds something that causes murder—as, for example, food or medicine.

Murder is contrary to natural law for the same reasons given in chapter 7 on the morality of suicide. It violates the right of the person to his or her life and the rights of the family, society and state, which have certain claims on the murdered person.

EUTHANASIA

Euthanasia, or mercy killing, has recently become a controversial topic in the United States. Recent interest in this issue has arisen with the practices of at least one physician in helping people to die. It has become even more controversial when coupled with the right to die or with death-with-dignity issues. Pulling the plug, so to speak, or turning off respirators when a person is brain-dead is at the heart of the controversy.

Is euthanasia moral or ethical? First, as Anthony Flew has pointed out,[5] the discussion is on *voluntary* euthanasia—that is, a person voluntarily requests death so as to escape an incurable disease or unbearable pain. Does that person have the right to ask to die? And if so, does the family, friends, physician or state have the duty to comply? There are different points of view.

Anthony Flew and Joseph Fletcher both claim that voluntary euthanasia is justified.[6] They pose a number of objections to which they respond and conclude that voluntary euthanasia is a shortening of life and the end—alleviation of suffering—justifies the means. They concur with Immanuel Kant that, in willing an end, a person is also willing the means. The end is good and the means to achieve it are not unethical in the case of euthanasia.

Others argue that if euthanasia involves the *direct* killing of a human being on one's own authority, it is murder. No person can voluntarily give up an inalienable right such as the right to life, and therefore no one else ordinarily has the right to take another's life unless self-defense is involved.

When is a person still a person? Courts of law and legislative bodies are currently dealing with this issue. If a person is brain-dead, some people claim that there is no human function anymore. They say that disconnecting a respirator is an indifferent act—neither good nor bad, and certainly not murder. Furthermore, they claim that a person has an obligation to take only ordinary care to preserve his or her life. Respirators and the like are *extraordinary* means of preserving life, therefore turning them off is at least an indifferent, if not a morally good, act.

While disconnecting a respirator involves a negative method of hastening death, giving drugs or injections that expedite death is a positive act. Fletcher and Flew do not distinguish between means. But many ethicists claim that such positive acts are immoral. Others state that the morality depends on whether the person is really a person—and if brain-dead already, a positive action is ethical.

The problem with these cases is that there is no general agreement on when death occurs. Does *death* mean cessation of the heart? Cessation of the brain? Or both? Science has been unable to resolve this issue. Civil laws have attempted to protect the rights of people and their families in such situations. Nevertheless, this is an example of a tertiary principle of natural law, which is not very clear. Even through deductive reasoning, it is difficult to arrive at a standard or principle that applies to all cases.

ABORTION

If issues such as euthanasia and the right to die or death with dignity are troublesome to ethicists, abortion presents an even greater dilemma. This is an issue that troubles most people, and affects administrators at all levels of government. Just as euthanasia raises the question of at which point death occurs, abortion involves the matter of when life begins. There is some agreement on the beginning of life as occurring in the third trimester of pregnancy; beyond that, there is little agreement on the beginning or definition of life among two diametrically opposed theories.

Andre Hellegers defines abortion as follows: "termination of pregnancy, spontaneously or by induction, prior to viability."[7] Obviously, spontaneous abortions or miscarriages are not subject to discussion in ethics, since they happen naturally or by accident. Ethics focuses on induced abortions. James C. Mohr provides a definition of induced abortion: "the intentional termination of gestation by any means and at any time from conception to full term."[8] Thus, it is the direct expulsion of the fetus from the womb of the pregnant woman before the fetus is capable of living outside the womb. Some people would eliminate the last part of the definition, "prior to viability" and concur with Mohr's definition as the direct expulsion of the fetus any time after conception and prior to birth. So the ethical problems concerning abortion begin with its definition.[9]

In addition to disagreements on the definition of abortion, there are differences in terminology.[10] For example, some pro-life writers always use the terms *infant* or *child* when talking about a fetus. John Noonan, in particular, uses these terms.[11] In contrast, pro-choice advocates do not use these terms until after birth. Likewise, pro-life forces use the term *mother* when speaking about a pregnant woman, and this implies that the unborn is a child or infant. Former President Reagan reflected this pro-life approach when he said: "I have often said when we talk about abortion, we are talking about two lives—the life of the mother and the life of the unborn child. Why else do we call a pregnant woman a mother?"[12] Yet *Webster's New Collegiate Dictionary* defines *mother* as "to give birth; to give rise to; produce." Not only is there no agreement on the morality of abortion, there is not even common language.

The ethical considerations regarding abortion focus on whether it is murder. Pro-life advocates claim that abortion is murder. The basis for this claim is their belief that human life begins at the moment of conception; therefore, any deliberate act to terminate the pregnancy is murder. Some pro-lifers also argue that science has established that life begins at the moment of conception.

Pro-choice advocates claim that nobody knows when human life begins and that science has not established, and is unable to establish, the exact time when life begins. They say that the only certainty is that life begins at birth. They cite the great philosophers—Aristotle, St. Augustine and St. Thomas Aquinas—in thinking that animation or the infusion of the human soul—the principle of life—begins eighty days after conception for females and forty days for males. They also cite the Catholic Church's vacillation on the morality of abortion over the past 700 years.[13] For pro-choicers, abortion is not murder. They say that it is preposterous for pro-lifers to equate the conception entity with personhood or with a thirty-nine-week-old fetus.

The philosophical issue of "personhood" enters the debate to the extent that pro-life forces claim that personhood, like animation, begins at conception. They say that, although Aristotle, Augustine, and Aquinas were great philosophers, they were poor physical or medical scientists. Pro-choice forces define personhood as "a thing that thinks" or, as John Locke claimed, something with knowledge of self; they say history denies that personhood begins until after birth. In *Roe v. Wade*, the U.S. Supreme Court seemed to concur with the pro-choice position.

Is abortion murder, and therefore immoral? Or is it moral? That is the basic issue. To most pro-lifers, abortion is murder unless performed to save the life of the woman. In such cases, the abortion is an act with two effects: the good, intended to save the woman's life; and the evil, unintended death of the fetus or unborn child. Some pro-life advocates would also permit abortion in cases of rape and incest. But this position is not logical if one maintains that life begins at conception and, regardless of the circumstances of conception, is still a human life and the taking of human life, including those resulting from rape and incest, cannot be justified. In other words, the feeling is that evil means do not justify a good end, regardless of the circumstances.

Teleological theorists may claim that the best we can do in abortion cases is to consider the circumstances, reflect on the options, weigh them carefully and decide the best outcome in every case. This results in different outcomes, with every outcome correct. It may be the same conclusion as reached by those who would allow abortion in cases of rape and incest, but teleologists arrive at that conclusion by a different process—reflection. They do not have absolute standards, such as those held by some pro-lifers. The teleological argument is more logical, a more sophisticated approach in the abortion debate.

Pro-choice advocates do not see most abortions as murder, but some have serious ethical problems with abortions performed in the third trimester, especially after determination of viability. Although few abortions are performed in the third trimester, it remains an issue for some pro-choice forces.

Pro-life advocates have determined that abortion is always or almost always immoral. If a person subscribes to this view, obviously he or she is bound to follow a certain conscience, as described in chapter 6. The argument is that abortion is contrary to natural law, and that civil laws permitting abortion are immoral and need not be obeyed; natural law is higher. Pro-life advocates often attempt to stop abortions from being performed by blocking access to abortion clinics or setting fire to or bombing the clinics. These are acts of civil disobedience, moral and ethical *provided the pro-life person feels that he or she is acting morally.* The previous chapter on conscience indicated that a person is bound to follow his or her certain conscience, even if erroneous and when invincible ignorance is not involved. But if a person has doubts about the correctness of his or her ethical position, those doubts should be resolved or vincible ignorance overcome before continuing the involvement. Thus, if pro-life advocates are certain that their actions are moral and they proceed with those actions, they will be acting illegally but morally in their view. They may end up in jail and pay large fines, but they will feel their actions were not unethical.

Likewise, pro-choice advocates, if they are convinced that their position is ethical—that abortion is not murder, and that civil laws clarify natural law—they must follow their conscience with actions that they also view as ethical. If they have doubts or are subject to vincible ignorance, they have an obligation to resolve those doubts or dispel the ignorance before further involvement.

Advocates of both pro-life and pro-choice engage in a considerable rhetoric, exaggeration, misrepresentation, distortion and perpetuation of myths.[14] If both sides engage in lying, the principles discussed earlier in this chapter for lying apply. Ethics cannot justify such tactics.

Abortion has become a great moral and political issue in the United States and in several other countries. But it was not always so, as discussed at length in *Women, Society, the State and Abortion.*[15] Likewise, arguments favoring or opposing abortion touch upon many factors other than ethics. Various authors have offered opposing views.[16] Arguments on both sides tend to be emotional rather than rational. Indeed, the arguments developed through reason are unlikely to convince either side, for both view abortion as a closed issue. For people ignorant of the real facts and issues, Robert Lane has said "Ignorance penalizes."[17] With both camps well established politically and with little rational communication, it is doubtful that anyone or any discipline can succeed in resolving this potentially soluble issue.

NOTES

1. Sissela Bok, *Lying: Moral Choices in Public and Private Life* (New York: Random House, 1978), p. 36.

2. Ibid.

3. Ibid., pp. 15, 37–39.

4. Ibid., pp. 154–73 See also Sissela Bok, *Secrets* (New York: Vintage, 1984).

5. Anthony Flew, "The Principle of Euthanasia," in *Morality in the Modern World*, Lawrence Habermehl, ed. (Encino, Calif.: Dickenson Publishing Company, 1976), pp. 238ff.

6. Ibid. Also, Joseph Fletcher, "Ethics and Euthanasia," in Habermehl, *Morality in Modern World*, pp. 249–56.

7. Andre E. Hellegers, "Abortion," in *Encyclopedia of Bioethics*, Warren T. Reich, ed. (New York: Free Press, 1978), p. 2.

8. James C. Mohr, *Abortion in America: The Origins and Evolution of National Policy, 1800–1900* (New York: Oxford University Press, 1978), p. viii.

9. Patrick J. Sheeran, *Women, Society, the State and Abortion: A Structuralist Analysis* (New York: Praeger, 1987), pp. 1–9.

10. Ibid., p. 69.

11. John T. Noonan, Jr., *A Private Choice* (New York: Free Press, 1979).

12. Ronald Reagan, *Abortion and the Conscience of the Nation* (New York: Thomas Nelson, 1984), p. 2.

13. Sheeran, *Women, Society*, pp. 49–89.

14. Ibid., pp. 115, 121.

15. Ibid., pp. 1–9, 57–99, 17.

16. See Tom L. Beauchamp, ed., *Ethics and Public Policy* (Englewood Cliffs, N.J.: Prentice-Hall, 1975); Daniel Callahan, *Abortion, Law, Choice, and Morality* (New York: Macmillan, 1970); Lawrence Habermehl, ed. *Morality in the Modern World* (Encino, Calif.: Dickenson Publishers, 1966), pp. 208–37; Noonan, *Private Choice*.

17. Robert E. Lane, *Political Ideology: Why the American Common Man Believes What He Believes* (New York: Free Press, 1962), p. 310.

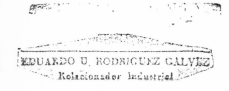

EDUARDO U. RODRIGUEZ GALVEZ
Relacionador Industrial

CHAPTER 9

Our Right to Private Property

In 1690, John Locke wrote his famous work, *Two Treatises of Government*.[1] Locke was the first to equate people's right to private property with their right to life and liberty. In fact, Locke emphasized that our right to private property existed in nature, before formation of the state. Thomas Hobbes, who wrote prior to Locke, also acknowledged private property as a human right, but a right conferred by the state.[2] Locke saw the creation of government only as a means of protecting people's right to private property.

The right to private property comes from the notion that external goods of the world, such as land and food, are for our use and benefit. Human beings need such goods to stay alive and fulfill a purpose. Every human being has an absolute right to use these goods. In a sense, then, they are common to all human beings, in that everyone can use them but no one is born with specific external goods. How do we acquire external goods? Through ownership. As Locke rightfully pointed out, it is wrong for a few people to possess all the material goods of the world and deprive others of them.

The issue of private ownership was a major factor for Karl Marx, and for the Soviet Union for over ninety years. Although less of an issue today, the roots of ownership merit ethical consideration. Ownership is closely associated with private enterprise, so it raises questions of private vs. public business. As such, it pertains to public administrators and their perception by both politicians and the public.

Ownership means that something belongs to a person or that a person has the right to it. A person who owns something has dominion over it. The right to ownership is an exclusive right to control and dispose of something as one's own. An owner may possess, use, change or do whatever else he pleases with things he owns as long as he does not violate the rights of others.

The object of ownership, or that which a subject may own, may be either material goods or immaterial goods such as the right to an invention, ownership of copyright, and so on. Another person, however, cannot be the object of ownership. Like all human rights, ownership exists with limitations. For example, one person can freely give another the ownership of a car, on a condition that the receiver provide the giver transportation once a week.

There are two kinds of ownership. Strictly speaking, *public ownership* refers to the power of the state to own goods for itself. But public ownership is broader than this. It also refers to the power the state has over all property, whereby it can dispose of a subject's property provided adequate compensation is paid to the owner and provided such disposal is for the common good. *Private ownership* is the power an individual or a group of people have over property or goods they possess.

The object of ownership is goods. There are three kinds of goods over which a person may have dominion:

1. Internal goods, or those that are part of our being, such as nature, life or human faculties.
2. External goods, or goods outside of ourselves. Human beings cannot own all external goods. They cannot own the external goods of other human beings or those of the state or those we have in common, such as air or water. Human beings can own only those external goods that they can effectively control, that are useful, that are limited and that are obtainable. External goods may be productive or those that produce other goods, such as machines. Nonproductive or consumable goods are those we destroy while using them, such as food.
3. Mixed goods are neither internal nor external, and include such things as honor or reputation.

The subject of ownership is any person or group of persons capable of exercising dominion over goods. This means that not only individuals but also organizations, both public and private, can own goods. In philosophical language, these are *moral persons*. First I discuss private ownership, then later in the chapter, public ownership.

PRIVATE OWNERSHIP

Do human beings have the right to own goods of all kinds and where does that right come from? There are different theories. Absolute communists maintain that human beings can own only consumable goods— that is, goods that we are here and now consuming. Doctrinaire socialists maintain that we cannot own any kinds of productive goods, such as land, factories or equipment. Agrarian socialists permit ownership of factories and equipment, but deny that land can be the object of ownership. Credit socialists forbid private ownership of credit, such as money. Other socialists permit private ownership of as many productive goods as an individual can personally work, but say a person has no right to own goods that he or she cannot effectively work personally.

While many philosophers and public administrators consider John Locke the father of private property, it was St. Thomas Aquinas who argued for people's right to private property. Aquinas wrote: "Man has the natural dominion of external goods because by reason and his will he can use external goods for his own utility in so much as these goods have been made for him."[3]

Aquinas's argument that people have dominion over external goods gives them a right to private property. If we have a right to these goods only at the moment of consuming them, this renders the right an illusion.

By our intellect, we can foresee future needs. We can foresee times of want, for which we must store food, protect crops and conserve fuel. We can foresee that times of illness and old age will make it difficult to provide ourselves with the necessities of life. We can foresee times of retirement when perhaps we want to develop ourselves culturally and intellectually. The only reasonable and natural way to provide for such occasions is through a natural right to productive goods. Furthermore, our desire for independence, to be master of our own destiny, argues for a right to private ownership, not only of consumable but also of productive goods.

Other philosophers have argued correctly that private ownership can be deduced from our right to the products of our own labor. We have from nature the unquestionable right to our own power and our own energy. The product of our labor is nothing more than our energy transformed. Thus, we can find the products of our labor in material goods, and we cannot separate them from the raw materials on which we exercise those powers. For instance, we cannot separate the power of the writer from his or her book or the carpenter from his or her product. The products of those labors or energies become an extension of the producer. We have a right to those things produced with our labor.

Aquinas argued that private ownership is necessary for society. He said that all of us are more careful with things that belong to us than what belongs to many or that we have in common. Besides, people tend to avoid labor or leave duties to others when things belong communally. Private ownership is a desirable state for society.

Aquinas argued that when we must provide for ourselves, we have more desirable human affairs. If everyone indiscriminately were to assume ownership of whatever he or she pleased, confusion would abound. Thus a system of private property is more desirable.

Finally, Aquinas points out that a system of private property ensures a peaceful society. In such a system everyone is more likely to be content with his or her own goods. In a system where people share common goods, disputes frequently arise.

Origins of the Right to Private Property

Theorists dispute the source of this right to private property. Two of the great contract theorists, Thomas Hobbes and Jean-Jacques Rousseau, held that the right to own private property arises from civil law—that is, the state confers that right on us. John Locke, the other great contract theorist, said the right to private property exists in the state of nature and is prior to the formation of states. Therefore, natural law confers this right on every human being. Pope Leo XIII, in his famous encyclical, "Rerum Novarum," concurred with Locke: "Every man by nature has the right to possess private property as his own. . . . He must not only have things that perish in the use, but also those which, though used, remain for use in the future."[4]

Although Locke equated the right to private property with the right to life and the right to liberty, it is doubtful if this natural right is as high on a scale of rights as the other two.

The Implications of Private Ownership

In the United States, ownership of private property is of great political importance. The Republican party places great emphasis on private property. It stresses ownership and opportunity to own as the chief means of economic development and as the solution to welfare dependency. However, while all human beings have the right to own private property, access to private property is not the same thing. In "Quadragessimo Anno," Pope Pius XI addressed the issue of private property:

This program [of acquiring private property] cannot, however, be realized unless the propertyless owner be placed in such circumstances that by skill and thrift he can acquire a certain moderate ownership. Every effort, therefore, must be made that at least in the future a just share of production be permitted to accumulate in the hands of the wealthy and that an ample sufficiency be supplied to the working men.[5]

Although he made this statement in 1931, we hear its echo from leaders of former Soviet bloc countries as well as from the Republican and Democratic candidates for the 1992 U.S. presidential campaign.

Are all human beings required to own private property? All human beings have the right to marry, but no individual is bound to marry, although many consider the institution of marriage essential for the well-being of the human race. Likewise, while nobody is bound to own private property, the system of private property is essential. In "Rerum Novarum," Pope Leo XIII said: "The law [the state] should favor ownership and its policy should be to induce as many people as possible to become owners."[6]

Private ownership offers several advantages, which are becoming obvious to leaders of former communist states: (1) it ensures more equitable distribution of property; (2) it attempts to bridge the gap between the rich and the poor; (3) it contributes to greater productivity because people tend to work harder when they work for themselves; and (4) it can result in lower migration because people who are satisfied tend to stay in their own countries. Although arguments favoring systems of private ownership are compelling, they do not provide answers for more equitable distribution of private property. Equitable distribution requires a massive public/private undertaking.

Private ownership brings with its benefits the corresponding duty to respect others' right to ownership. This means that stealing or deliberately destroying another's property is unethical. But what if a person is starving? Is it ethical or moral to steal food to stay alive?

Obviously, there is a clash of rights. Undoubtedly, the right to life is greater than the right to private property. In addition, some philosophers maintain that, in such instances, all private property becomes common. But in either case, most philosophers maintain that it is not unethical to steal to prevent starvation. Nevertheless, it may be illegal, and the offender may well go to jail for breaking civil law that protects another's right to private property.

PUBLIC OWNERSHIP

While private ownership is a natural right and should be the prevailing system, natural law does not forbid public ownership. In "Quadragessimo Anno," Pope Pius XI noted: "It is rightly contended that certain forms of property must be reserved for the state since they carry with them an opportunity for dominion too great to be left to private individuals without injury to the community at large."[7] This reiterates the principle that private property should prevail in our society.

In general, the state can own all it needs materially to carry out its duties and to ensure the independence and prosperity of people within its jurisdiction. If the state engages in total or indiscriminate nationalization, it violates the principle of private ownership, and such nationalization is unethical.

Limited nationalization may be ethical under two conditions. The first is based on the primacy of private ownership. Since the citizen has a natural right to own property, the state must not nationalize *all* the means of production, either in one act or gradually. The second condition comes from the nature and purpose of the state itself. The right of the state to own property does not come from majority vote, nor from the idea that the state is superhuman. The right of the state to own property derives from the fact that the state (as the next chapter discusses) is an institution demanded by natural law. Therefore, the state may own whatever it needs to promote the welfare of its citizens. But that is limited ownership, and the state may not go beyond that degree of ownership without approaching the unethical.

Since people constitute the state, and since people and political parties often disagree on what is needed to promote the welfare of the citizens, as well as what will be needed in the future, it is often difficult to assess what may be ethical or unethical. Undoubtedly, hoarding large amounts of property that private citizens could use may be an unethical state practice.

Executive Order 12803, signed by President George Bush on April 30, 1992, addresses privatization. The opposite of nationalization, privatization, involves the release of public property for private ownership. Every federal executive department and agency, "to the extent permitted by law," will review procedures that facilitate and promote the privatization by sale or long-term lease of many publicly owned assets. It appears that infrastructure assets such as roads, bridges, tunnels, airports, schools, prisons and hospitals are among such assets. The transfer of these assets to the private sector offers profit-making potential for the private sector and income for the nation. As to how much of this privatization will occur and how well the private sector can handle these assets is another matter. But the executive order conforms to Lockean philosophy and accepted principles of ownership.

What Assets Does the State Need to Promote the Welfare of Its Citizens?

In the United States this is a controversial issue rooted in the political philosophies of Thomas Hobbes, John Locke and Jean-Jacques Rousseau. It is an issue that focuses on the extent and role of government. It is an issue that separates liberals from conservatives, Democrats from Republicans.

Hobbes saw government as good and necessary to protect ourselves from ourselves and others. Locke viewed government as serving a limited role, primarily solving disputes and protecting private property. The saying "the government that governs least governs best" has its roots in Locke. Although Hobbes and Locke were both classical liberals and promoters of radical individualism, the United States has largely subscribed to Locke's philosophy of limited government.

Lockean philosophy on the sanctity of private property and the limitation of government affects public administrators, particularly in the United States. Governments in general, and the federal government in particular, are not beloved institutions. The public does not have much admiration or respect for civil servants. The Reagan and to a certain extent the Bush administrations have often cited the importance of the private sector while maligning the public sector. Reagan saw the root cause of our economic and social problems in an oversized federal government. These views of government often negatively affect civil servants, who constitute the machinery of government. If government in general is bad, and big government in particular is the source of our problems, then public employees are the cause of these problems. But even Locke recognized the need for some government and some civil servants.

If the individual and the private sector are the solution to our problems, the programs proposed and administered by civil servants must be evil. At best, such programs are suspicious. So it is difficult for dedicated civil servants to be enthusiastic about the programs for which they are responsible. Public administrators should be mindful that, as long as the private sector holds philosophical superiority, it will never have great affection for public administrators. It is also important to note, however, that private industries sometimes fail and that the public sector must come to the rescue. Even the most conservative politicians recognize that "the invisible hand" does not always prevail, and that there is a genuine need for government employees.

The major question is what and how much government is needed to fulfill its role of ensuring the independence and prosperity of its citizens. Politicians have different views on how to address the needs of the state. Based on Lockean philosophy and the words of Pope Pius XI quoted above, we can determine some of the things the state needs to carry out its mission. The state needs certain materials and services to govern, such as office buildings, legislative houses and courts of law as well as the furnishings and equipment to operate these facilities. Likewise, the state needs the services of civil servants, law enforcement and military personnel to meet its responsibilities, though the number and calibre of civil servants is controversial.

The state must also ensure that the country's natural resources are put to good use. On this issue, the role of the state is as subsidiary—that is, it must watch, direct, promote and restrain. Only when private enterprise is unavailable or resources are being abused should the state intervene. State intervention is justified when private owners do not exist or when private ownership would be dangerous. For instance, when private owners do not exist, state ownership occurs by default. The state intervenes because private owners do not have the capital, they lack interest or they fear lack of profit. If private developers are unwilling, uninterested or fear losses by building houses, the state may have to step in. Likewise, building roads or large water-control schemes may be such that state intervention is necessary. However, nationalization or complete ownership by the state is the last resort, since the state's role is to direct and motivate the private sector, not do things itself.

The role of the state, then, is to motivate private enterprise to take action. The state can help private enterprise through subsidies and incentives. The U.S. government has gone beyond initial funding by providing subsidies to local governments and private enterprises to keep them from going bankrupt. This appears to be reasonable and ethical. But if forced into what is normally private business, the state should make only a temporary effort, until such time as the business can go back to private ownership.

State ownership can also originate as a precaution when private ownership might be dangerous to the community. For instance, it might be dangerous to allow a private enterprise to own military nuclear weapons. Various industries that provide the community with goods or services of vital importance, or which require community control, may be subject to state ownerhsip. Obviously, government and private enterprise have different views on this and propose different policies and practices. When private enterprises form monopolies, establishing high prices that leave the community at their mercy, the state may be justified in taking over these monopolies if it cannot break them up.

Since both government and the private sector may own property, what about joint state-corporate ownership? Obviously, such ventures are possible and sometimes necessary; it is more desirable to have these partnerships than total nationalization. Although private ownership is the ideal, in some cases a public-private joint venture may be the only or best situation.

In conclusion, I state that it is unethical for a government to nationalize *all* the means of production. Limited nationalization may sometimes be ethical if the private sector is unable to carry out those tasks. There are certain industries and services, because of their extraordinary importance and for the common good, may legitimately and ethically be nationalized.

When a state takes over a private enterprise or acquires private property, just compensation must be paid. It is difficult to determine what a just price is. Undoubtedly, public administrators can help arrive at these determinations, although often there are political, social and ethical considerations involved in addition to economics.

Most democratic societies subscribe to John Locke's right to private ownerhsip and the sanctity of private property. The philosophies of Marx and Lenin, however, are different. But with the demise of Soviet communism beginning toward the end of 1989, the Soviet Union and many Eastern European countries have abandoned the state-mandated economy and embraced the notion of capitalism and private ownership.

OBLIGATIONS ARISING FROM PRIVATE OWNERSHIP

Private ownership bears certain obligations and duties. For example, owners must not violate the legitimate rights of others. Stealing, cheating or destroying the property of others is unethical. These are violations of others' rights, which we have a duty to respect. Based on our natural right to private ownership, we can deduce certain principles that are applicable to owners. One of the chief obligations of owners is to provide employment for others, so that they too may acquire the necessities of life and pursue their natural right to private ownership. In addition, the private sector must pay just wages and set just prices and rents. This is not an easy matter, and the "invisible hand" is not always a reliable mechanism. Too often the corporate world "rips off" the public.

Social obligations also flow from the concept of private ownership and private enterprise. For instance, there is an obligation to help the less fortunate. Sometimes corporations respond positively to this obligation; frequently they donate a portion of their profits or surplus goods. Although such efforts are praiseworthy, they are no excuse for unethical behavior.

Private owners have an obligation also to use their right of ownership for the common good. This is particularly true if we take the view that the state should not be involved in the production and delivery of most goods and services. But it is often difficult for the private sector to balance the need for profit with meeting the common good. Therefore, the state often must determine what is the common good. Public administrators, in holding a neutral status, can play an important role in determining what is the common good.

Taxation is a major issue in the United States. It should be no surprise that those who favor less government are opposed to increased taxes. "Read my lips. No new taxes," said George Bush in the 1988 presidential campaign. Taxes are one of the principal ways of supporting government programs. But if the government were not providing services or operating industries, there would be no need for more taxes. If government were kept small, only a small amount of taxes would be needed to support government endeavors.

But while the private sector has obligations, it often does not meet these obligations. Therefore, some government programs are needed to serve the common good, and taxes help finance these endeavors. Should the rich and the private sector pay more taxes? Some people say yes while others maintain it is not fair to penalize those who have become rich. The best answer is that everyone should pay his or her *fair share* of taxes. But determining what is fair is difficult. Former California governor Jerry Brown, while a candidate for the Democratic party nomination in the 1992 presidential campaign, proposed a flat tax whereby everyone except the very poor would pay the same percentage of income tax, without deductions and loopholes currently available to the more affluent. Although he did not spell out the details, he raised an issue of fairness that may lead to future debate.

People who are unable to work, have no material goods or are unable to obtain help from family members or relatives poses serious problems for society. Who should provide help for the homeless? It is clear that society has an obligation to help. If the private sector can provide assistance, that is acceptable. If it cannot or does not, obviously the state must intervene; hence, there is a need for some state programs of assistance. And that means there is a need for taxes to support these endeavors. Indeed, the state may be the best—and perhaps the only—entity capable of providing services of this kind for the common good.

But what if the state is also unable to provide these services? What can the disadvantaged do? Ethicists distinguish between the right to own private property and the right use or abuse of private property. The right to own private property does not cease, regardless of whether a person uses it well or abuses it. But when neither the private nor public sector provides for the disadvantaged, the disadvantaged may take the super-fluous goods of the rich in order to sustain life. This principle of morality comes from consideration of the apparent conflict between rights. The right to life is higher than the right to private property. Stealing in this case is not stealing in the strict sense, because in such dire necessity, superfluous goods become common goods and their use to sustain life is a good act. Once again, the person who takes such goods may go to jail for theft. This illustrates the difference between morality and legality.

However, this does not mean that the owner of the stolen property has lost his or her rights to that property—only that the owner has lost access to it. Pope Leo XIII, in "Rerum Novarum," said that the government may determine what is in the interest of the common good if natural law has not specifically defined it, provided that the definition of the government does not violate other principles of natural law.[8]

INDIVIDUALISM VS. COLLECTIVISM

The foregoing discussion illustrates the primacy of private ownership. In fact, private ownership is a compromise between two extremes—individualism and collectivism. While arguments favoring private owner-ship and private property are convincing, these rights are not without duties and obligations. If private ownership is bereft of social obligations, the theory is individualism. If, on the other hand, we reject the individual character of private ownership, we identify with the theory of collectivism. Individualism is the theory of ethicists on the far right and collectivism is the theory of those on the far left. I briefly discuss both as extremes of the right of ownership.

Individualism

Individualism was a reaction to mercantilism, a system that followed feudalism in Europe. It held that governments should regulate all industries for the common good. The classical theorists—Hobbes, Locke and Rous-seau—writing in reaction to mercantilism, acknowledged the individual's right to private property. Locke saw the right as coming directly from natural law, but Hobbes and Rousseau held that the right came from the state. Nevertheless, all recognized the importance of the individual, with full and unrestricted liberty. *Laissez-faire* ("let the people do as they please") summarizes the theory of individualism. In contrast, "Let the state regulate" summarizes the theory of mercantilism.

According to individualism, in business there must be complete liberty for the individual. There must be free trade, freedom to negotiate contracts, freedom to determine compensation, and freedom from interference from all sources. The motto of individualism was "Every man for himself" and accumulation of the greatest amount of property. The best means of achieving this was by free trade. This was the theory of Adam Smith, John Stuart Mill and Jeremy Bentham.

Unfortunately, individualism resulted in dreadful evils, through the promotion of inordinate selfishness and greed. It helped destroy weaker businesses and ensured concentration of wealth in the hands of a few. It resulted in long working hours and in child labor in deplorable conditions. There was degradation and virtual slavery of workers.

This system prevailed during the Industrial Revolution. There was no concern for the common good. There was no interest in the unfortunate. There was no government intervention of any kind. Profit and gain were the only goals worth pursuing. This was a theory of private ownership all right, but without social and ethical concerns.

Collectivism

Collectivism was a reaction to individualism. Its purpose was to cure the evils wrought by individualism, abolishing the system of private ownership—or at least ownership over the means of production—and substituting the community as possessor and dispenser of material goods. Other names for collectivism are communism or socialism, although there are some distinctions.

Collectivism maintains that the highest goal for humankind is material property. People have nothing spiritual in them. They can only fully obtain material property by collective ownership. Individuals will not own; a collection of people is the true owner. The individual exists only for society, which concerns itself only with the production and distribution of goods. To this society the individual must give everything, including labor. Society based on a committee of experts plans the best way to use human beings to produce goods and also provides for every material need. People have no rights in this society; they do what society tells them to do, they fulfill the tasks assigned them. This society is not unlike the one that Rousseau's General Will envisions.[9]

Nevertheless, there is some confusion as to what constitutes society in collectivism. Some claim it is the state; others maintain it is a new form of society yet to be developed or a syndicate of industries unified into national groups. A third view sees society as a vast group of workers joined together, working for the good of all and freely taking the goods they produce. In this perception, there is no state because workers will have overthrown the state.

In contrast, *communism* gives complete ownership of all goods, both productive and consumable, to the whole community. The community ensures, through expert administrators, that production of goods is achieved, that there is suitable variety and abundance, and that every person receives what he or she needs.

Socialism differs only slightly from communism. Socialism allows individuals to own consumable goods and perhaps such productive goods as the individual can manage. But there must be collective and undivided ownership of all sources, means of production and distribution of goods. Only such items as food, clothing and the like are exempt from common ownership. There must also be common administration of all activities by which workers produce goods. The administration is responsible for determining products by kind and variety, value, prices, wages, equipment needed, distribution methods and place. The unit of administration may be national, state or local government, or a combination thereof. But the state is not political, it is democratic and economic. It administers things, not people.

Collectivism, communism and socialism have noteworthy proponents—they consider Plato as one of the early advocates. In addition, the Acts of the Apostles in the New Testament states that the early Christians "had all things in common." In *Utopia*, Sir Thomas More advocated a similar system. Subscribers to the general theory of collectivism in the last century include Saint Simon in France, Robert Owen in England and Marx and Engels in Germany.

The discussion of ownership earlier in this chapter argued that the right to private ownership comes from natural law. There were arguments to show that this right results in better interest in and production of material goods. In addition, people are not cogs in the wheel of the state, as collectivism would make them. Rather, they are people with certain natural rights and duties. Further, as discussed in chapter 3 regarding psychology, people are not purely material beings (which collectivism maintains), but composed of a body and a spirit.

Although collectivism argues that all people are created equal and should therefore equally share in the goods of the earth, there are flaws in that argument. It is true in the abstract that people are created equal, because everyone has the same natural rights. But in concrete cases this does not hold. An individual may not enjoy the same natural rights as another. For example, some people choose to marry, others do not. Some choose to own property whereas others, such as monks through a vow of poverty, choose not to. Besides, human beings differ from one another in physique, natural ability, talent, taste and health. So the collectivist argument does not hold on the issue of equality. Collectivism is not so compelling as to disregard the right to ownership and private property.

Karl Marx (1818–1883)

Although most scholars of philosophy and politics acknowledge that communism or Marxism has failed in Europe in recent times, it is a conceptually interesting and a historic development to merit brief consideration here. While Karl Marx is generally acknowledged as the developer of the theory of communism, it was his contemporary and fellow countryman, Friedrich Engels, who popularized Marx's theory. Marx was also a follower of this great German idealist, and early in his life also espoused Hegel's philosophy of idealism. During those days, Marx saw people as confined to "a psychic prison" of their own making, from which they must free themselves. The "mature" Marx saw people as constrained, not by a prison of their own making but by capitalism. People must revolt to gain freedom.[10] Marx spelled out his theory on communism mostly in two books, *The Communist Manifesto*, published in 1848, and *Das Kapital*, published in 1867.

In these two major publications, Marx set out to prove why socialism must inevitably come. Relying on Hegel's notion that progress or evolution occurs when an idea we have (called a thesis) conflicts with an opposite idea (antithesis). This conflict produces a third idea, the synthesis.

Rejecting Hegel's idealism, Marx claimed that everything in the world is material functioning according to fixed laws—not just artifacts of consciousness. One principle governs all human relations; the production of means to support life and the exchange of things produced. For production, people need labor, skill and instruments. These are "productive forces." Production involves relations between people and those he called "productive relations."

Marx explained how socialism or communism must come about. In the first stage of history there was complete anarchy, when productive forces and productive relations were not regulated. Marx—using Hegel's notion of thesis, antithesis and synthesis—showed that anarchy gave way to slavery, when a few people controlled the productive forces and relations and the rest were slaves. Through the synthesis came the new state of feudalism, when people were serfs, not slaves, but politically unfree. By the same process, feudalism gave way to capitalism, when there were a few great owners but the majority were workers who were politically unfree. Soon, by the same process of thesis, antithesis and synthesis, capitalism would give way to socialism, when all people would own and all would be free. That final stage would occur through a class struggle between those who have and those who do not. The dictatorship of the proletariate would be final. It would result in a classless society—the final goal of the evolution.

In addition to this historical progression, Marx also focused on the notion of "surplus value" to show why socialism must inevitably replace capitalism. According to Marx, all value has its source in labor: labor creates all value. All goods, however, have two values: "use value," or the value of the good to the user, and "exchange value," or that for which you can exchange something. Exchange value is the only value of importance. What gives an object its exchange value? It is not, he said, its size, weight or shape because these are not common to all things. The value of all goods must be something all of them have in common. And the labor required to produce goods is normally what these goods have in common. Labor is, therefore, the creator of exchange value and labor must get all the value it creates.

But labor does not get all its value because capitalists continue to rob workers of their wealth. The wages workers receive are *only part of the value they create*. After workers have created the exchange value corresponding to their wages, the capitalist compels them to work additional hours during which they accumulate additional exchange value over and above the actual wages. This Marx called "surplus value," which capitalists take to enrich themselves at the expense of the workers.

Such exploitation of workers will inevitably produce a dictatorship of the proletariate. As the exploited—who have never themselves exploited anyone—grow and become more united, they will seize power. Then there will be only one class—the workers. There will be no more exploitation because workers will own what they produce and there will be an abundance of provisions for all. In the final stage, dissolution of the state will occur through formation of the industrial directorate, leading eventually to the final stage of progress—the dictatorship of the proletariate.

In Marx's view, there is no need for ethics or religion in the final stage, because these distract people from gaining the highest degree of material comfort. Religion has preached patience under hardship, and ethics subscribes to submission to lawful authority. Ethics and religion are the result of the productive system of the time and will disappear with capitalism.

It is obvious that Marx's prediction that the state will fade away has not occurred and that it is unlikely to occur. Likewise, society as well as capitalism continue. The next chapter examines the nature of society and the state.

NOTES

1. John Locke, *Two Treatises of Government*, Peter Laslett, ed. (New York: Cambridge University Press, 1960).

2. Thomas Hobbes, *The Leviathan*, Michael Oakeshott, ed. (New York: Macmillan, 1962).

3. Thomas Aquinas, *Summa Theologica*, Secunda Secundae Art. I and II.

4. Pope Leo XIII, "Rerum Novarum," *The Papal Encyclicals*, Anne Fremantle, ed. (New York: New American Library, 1956), pp. 168–69.

5. Pope Pius XI, "Quadragessimo Anno," *The Papal Encyclicals*, Anne Fremantle, ed. (New York: New American Library, 1956), p. 234.

6. Pope Leo XIII, *Papal Encyclicals*, p. 170.

7. Pope Pius XI, *Papal Encyclicals*, p. 232.

8. Pope Leo XII, *Papal Encyclicals*, p. 172.

9. Jean-Jacques Rousseau, *The Social Contract and Discourse on the Origin of Inequality*, Lester G. Crocker, ed. (New York: Washington Square Press, 1967), pp. 30ff.

10. Gibson Burrell and Gareth Morgan, *Sociological Paradigms and Organizational Analysis* (Portsmouth, N.H.: Heinemann, 1985), pp. 33–34, 326–33.

CHAPTER 10

Social Ethics—Our Rights and Duties as Members of Society

Previous chapters addressed the rights and duties of human beings to themselves and others. This chapter focuses on human beings as members of society. Society has been defined as a stable union of two or more people for a common purpose, to be achieved by common action. Theorists use a similarly broad definition for an organization.

Human beings are not just rational animals; we are also social beings. We have a natural desire and need for one another. This is instinctive or derived from natural law. There are two societies of particular importance to human beings: the family and the state.

THE SOCIETY OF THE FAMILY

President Reagan and his Republican administration came to Washington, D.C., in 1981 with, among other things, a major focus on the family and family values. For that administration, it was almost as if they had discovered something new—the family. But the family is nothing new to ethics, where it has been the subject of study and debate for centuries. There is no doubt that the make-up of the family and family values has changed in the United States over the past several decades. It was Reagan policy to restore the family and family values to the pedestal from which the administration claimed it had fallen. By strengthening the family, the administration hoped to strengthen the nation as a whole. A strong family is also what ethics promotes. The Bush administration continued to make the family and family values a major policy issue. Conservatives generally talk about "traditional values" or a universal code of values, some of which are applicable to the family. But it is unclear what they mean by *values* or *traditional*. It is also unclear what this so-called universal code of values consists of, whose values it contains or who has consented to it. Some people have claimed that the term "family values" is often not supported by programs that encourage whatever those values are.

The word *value* means "a belief, standard, criteria, or preference that is held by an individual." It is also possible for groups of individuals to share values. St. Thomas Aquinas, however, had this to say on the matter: *"Quot sunt personae, tot sunt opiniones"* ("There are as many opinions as there are people"). When the word *moral* is tacked on to values, the implication is that there are right and wrong values. Columnist Ellen Goodman thinks that conservatives define moral values too narrowly: "Conservatives tend to define moral values in the narrow context of sex."[1] This seems also to be St. Augustine's approach to moral values. However, most conservatives deny this allegation. At the same time, some of them pay little attention to values that do not have some kind of sexual connection.

Ethicists have shown profound interest in family values. They see the family as the basic or fundamental unit of society. Ethics examines the needs of this unit by looking at its structure and examining the rights and duties of members of that structure. In this way, ethics leads to a set of principles that spell out values for the family. Some may call these traditional values. Ethics, however, examines all the rights and duties of the family and its members. It does not engage in empty rhetoric. Unfortunately, the ideal family that ethics portrays is often not the modern American family. Nevertheless, the rights and duties of family members do not cease, even when the family is not the ideal or traditional one.

The family is a society because all other societies trace their roots to the family and derive their membership from it. In its most elementary form, domestic society is conjugal society, or the union of a man and woman in marriage. Marriage is a recognized union between a man and a woman. The purpose of such a union is to beget and educate children. With the birth of children, the conjugal society of marriage becomes the family society. Traditionally, *conjugal society* refers to a permanent union of a man and woman, formed for the purpose of begetting and educating children. St. Thomas Aquinas, John Locke and many other philosophers considered parents of great importance as educators of their children.

Unity and Indissolubility

The definition of marriage has two qualities: unity and indissolubility. Philosophers have argued that natural law gives the quality of unity to marriage. *Unity* means that a man and a woman should only be married to each other at the same time. This excludes polygyny, whereby one man may have several wives, or polyandry, where one woman may have several husbands. Philosophers attribute the quality of unity to marriage because they feel that polygyny and polyandry are unnatural, or contrary to natural law. If the purposes of marriage are perpetuation and education of the human species, mutual happiness and respect for one another, the union of one man and one woman seems best and most natural. In particular, since education of children is a responsibility of both parents, a monogamous union appears to me to be the most appropriate way to accomplish this end. It is not impossible for these duties to be carried out by one parent, but human reason tells us it is easier when there are two parents. In a monogamous union, identification of the true parents and their joint responsibilities are also easier.

The quality of *indissolubility* means that the marriage union is permanent, or lasting. The argument supporting indissolubility focuses again on the education of children. A permanent union provides a stable environment for nurturing and educating children. Thus, when there are children involved, I believe that an indissoluble union is logical and necessary. But when there are no children involved or when the children have left the stable environment of the home, the quality of indissolubility has less merit. Also, when the children are abused or neglected, does indissolubility of the marriage union make sense? Hardly, because the purpose of educating and providing security is violated. Therefore, for the safety, security and education of the children as well as the other spouse, the state may grant divorces as separations.

In the United States, divorce is commonplace. While the ideal is marriage until the death of one of the partners, this is not reality. A greater need, a greater good—the security and education of the children and the happiness of the partners—often takes precedence. Divorce, then, may be truly the best and most ethical way to resolve matrimonial acrimony. Couples contemplating marriage should continue to look on it as a union with the qualities of unity and indissolubility. However, those who enter into prenuptial agreements stipulating what each should get should a divorce occur are acting more realistically, albeit less romantically.

Dissolution of marriages often brings with it pain and grief. Public administrators and officials involved in prenuptial agreements, divorce proceedings or family aid programs often can help to make the best of a bad situation. Divorce and family court officials as well as social workers have a serious responsibility to ensure equity. Professionalism and impartiality are key qualities for those involved with divorce proceedings. Issues such as who gets custody of the children, procedures for joint custody or amount of child support and alimony require professional skills tempered with fairness and impartiality. Regardless of how you may personally feel about the divorce or the personalities involved, you have an obligation to carry out, with the highest ethical considerations, the requirements of the law and the decrees of the judicial system.

Rights and Duties of the Family Society

As mentioned earlier, with the birth of a child, the conjugal society becomes the family society. This is the society that exists between parents and their children. It is the society that provides nourishment, security and education for children. It is a natural society—a society emanating from natural law—because men and women have a natural desire to marry and establish a family. The primary purpose of the family, however, is the welfare of children. A secondary purpose is the happiness of the members of the family. To achieve these two ends, there are mutual rights and duties involved.

Parents have the right and duty to provide for the bodily needs of their children. This includes providing food, clothing and other necessities of life. Parents are also responsible for the education of their children. This pertains not only to formal education but also to development of the child's personality, values, and ethical principles. Parents are the primary educators of their children. This right springs from the fact that parents are the immediate cause of their child's existence. On the other hand, children have a right to be cared for, trained and educated by their parents. Corresponding to that right, children have a duty to love, respect and obey their parents. Whether or not a child is conceived in marriage, and regardless of whether it is a one- or two-parent family, the parent's obligations and duties do not cease. Most single parents are women; in 1992, there were 10.1 million single mothers in the United States.[1] Although the traditional family, with a husband and a wife, has been changing, the ethical principles governing the rights and duties of the parents do not cease.

THE RIGHT TO WORK AND TO EARN A JUST WAGE

Everyone has the right to start a family and to provide for it. Since workers are members of society, they have a right to work, as pointed out in chapter 7. This means they have a right to a job that will enable them to provide for themselves and their families. But in addition to the right to work, workers have the right to a just wage in exchange for that labor.

Just Wage vs. Living Wage

A *living wage* is income sufficient to keep a person alive. It allows a person to live in a fitting manner according to his or her dignity as a human being. It may be the minimum wage that allows a worker to attain food, clothing and shelter; meet health care and education needs; and enjoy reasonable recreation—all with some provision for the future.

But when a person is married and has a family, a living wage will not suffice to provide the support the family needs. Human reason, regardless of its limitations, can deduce that the family needs a just wage. A just wage is more than a living wage because the family has greater obligations and more responsibilities than the individual. The "Iron Law of Wages" of economists in the nineteenth century maintained that supply and demand fixed all wages. As a result, this Iron Law of Wages was one of the reasons Karl Marx developed his socialism. It also led to the great encyclical "Rerum Novarum," by Pope Leo XIII in 1891, and forty years later to the encyclical "Quadragessimo Anno" by Pope Pius XI. With a philosophical basis these two encyclicals spell out a person's right to work and to be paid a just wage.

The Ethics of Strikes

The right to form associations or unions, is a natural right spelled out in the 1891 and 1941 encyclicals. But does membership in such unions also grant members the right to strike? Before addressing this question it is useful to define a strike. A *strike* is the act by organized workers of ceasing work in order to force an employer to grant higher wages or better benefits or working conditions. Laying aside until later in this chapter the issue of public workers, it is clear that workers have the right to strike in some situations.

Some strikes are ethical, while others are not. What makes a strike ethical? The principles governing self-defense given in chapter 7 are applicable to strikes. A strike is ethical if the following conditions are present:

1. There must be just cause to cease work, owing to the hardships that will result for the employer as well as for the workers, customers and sometimes the community. It is often difficult to determine what just cause is, although wages, contracts, benefits and working conditions are often the main issues. The assumption is that these constitute just or reasonable cause.

2. A strike must be the last resort, not the first. Because of the potential hardships, every peaceful effort toward negotiation must have been tried and failed.

3. There must be reasonable hope of success on the part of the strikers. If there is little or no hope, strikers are not justified in inflicting additional hardship on themselves and others.

4. The advantages to be gained must outweigh the disadvantages. Otherwise, the strike is a futile exercise.

5. The strike should not violate a valid contract. If such a contract is in place, it is unethical to strike because of the sacred nature of that contract.

6. The strikers must make every effort to avoid violence.

Applying these principles to a few specific strikes enables us to make the following judgments:

1. A sitdown strike is usually unethical because it is not ethical to occupy an employer's property against the employer's will.

2. A sympathetic strike, or a strike initiated out of sympathy (not grievance) for other workers, may be either ethical or unethical. It is ethical when the sympathy is itself a just strike and the sympathizers violate no existing contract; otherwise, it may be unethical.

3. A general strike, when workers in all industries cease work, is very rarely justified because of the difficulty in fulfilling the six conditions, especially in compensating for the hardships and inconveniences suffered by the entire community.

4. A lockout strike, or when the employer does not allow workers access to their jobs, may be either ethical or unethical. It is ethical if the employer is protesting unjust demands, but it is often difficult to assess what and when demands are unjust.

5. A jurisdictional strike, usually called because unions are disputing among themselves, is usually unethical because such strikes cannot meet the six conditions stated above.

Because of the natural right of workers to unionize and to strike in at least some situations, and because of the hardships that strikes normally bring, it is the duty of the state to prevent strikes by mediation—and at times prohibit them by law. Before elaborating further, it is necessary to consider what the state is, what its purpose is, its origin and its powers.

THE SOCIETY OF THE STATE

Just as it is natural for people to form the family or domestic society, it is likewise natural to form the civil society or the state. The state is a large society comprising many families working in cooperation for the common good under the authority of the ruler. The state is a natural society because people have a natural aptitude, urge and need to associate with others to attain happiness. No family is self-supporting, but families linked together can support themselves. The state is such a combination of families. This reasoning leads to the conclusion that natural law demands the existence of a state.

Not all philosophers accept this conclusion. Thomas Hobbes maintained that people's original condition in the state of nature was warfare.[2] The state is an artificial creation to ensure self-preservation. John Locke, while disagreeing with Hobbes, said that the state is artificial, established by people to resolve disputes over private property. Jean-Jacques Rousseau claimed that people in the natural state were happy, but gradually fraud and deceit entered society and people formed the state by social contract to restore peace.[3] Evolutionists claim that, just as people developed from animals by blind force, these same blind forces also produced the state.

The Purpose of the State

The purpose of the state is to serve the common good, the public welfare, peace and prosperity. The state exists for the good of its citizens. Since families make up the state, the state exists to help families. States exist to help people do what they are unable to do for themselves. This is the principle of subsidiarity—that the state should never do for its citizens what the citizens can do for themselves. In practice, that means that the state should help its citizens only when they need help. It should supplement, not supplant. In this capacity, the state is acting for the common good.

It is the duty of the state to protect the community from its enemies, to make laws and to administer justice. The state must provide a proper or suitable education system. It must regulate commerce so that the community will not be at the mercy of a few individuals. It should maintain a suitable physical and moral climate conducive to the needs of the citizens.

In summary, the state exists for its citizens, as opposed to the totalitarian view that citizens exist for the state.

To function in this capacity, the state must have authority and/or jurisdiction. *Authority* is the right and power to put an obligation on citizens to carry out the common good. *Jurisdiction* means that the state has the power to legislate, to administer the laws and to enforce them. These are legislative, executive and judicial powers. Theorists who maintain that the state comes from natural law see jurisdiction as coming directly from natural law and indirectly from God, the author of natural law.

How do rulers acquire jurisdiction? There are three theories. Thomas Hobbes and many others subscribed to the divine right of kings. This theory maintained that God gave rulers authority by a special act, and so these rulers govern by divine law. In his *First Treatise on Government*, John Locke sufficiently refuted this theory.

A second idea, called the transfer theory, says that authority comes from natural law to the people, and the people in turn give it by consent to a particular person or group. This theory is somewhat consistent with the ideas of Locke and Rousseau. A third theory is the Designation Theory. The people designate the ruler by some method, and the ruler after designation receives the authority to rule from God.

Who Is the Ruler?

How does the state carry out its functions and duties? How does it protect and defend its citizens, provide education, administer justice? Chapter 9 addressed the state's right to own property, equipment and materials to carry out some duties and responsibilities. It also showed how the state needs the services of people—civil servants, administrators, teachers, police, military personnel, legislators, judges—to carry out the functions of the government. Public administrators are the state, they are the government.

Since the state exists for the common good and the welfare of its citizens, civil servants must subscribe to the notion of the common good. Their actions are not those of private citizens. Their actions are public actions. They must subscribe to a higher morality than the private citizens. Civil servants and public administrators are not the masters of ordinary citizens; rather, they are their servants. Some would say they should be the slaves of the citizens, but *servant* seems to describe adequately the roles of civil workers and public administrators.

Since civil servants and public administrators are the government, they are subject to the same controversy and criticisms as are democratic governments. Those who subscribe to Thomas Hobbes's notion of government, or "bold state," as Richard Stillman calls it, see the government as good, necessary and doer of everything. Those who subscribe to the John Locke, Adam Smith, John Stuart Mill philosophy of limited government, or what Stillman calls "no state," often despise the government and its representatives.[4] And public administrators, often by lording over citizens and failing to carry out their duties, bring additional criticism and even hatred upon themselves.

As a result, the public often sees public servants as "faceless people who operate from windowless rooms" or as "faceless functionaries."[5] Thomas Sowell, a conservative economist at the Hoover Institution, in the *Washington Times*, summed up public service as follows:

The biggest part of the "public service" sector is government. . . . A more profound problem is that many of the intelligentsia, political "leaders" and the morally anointed see themselves as special people who should be overriding the demands expressed through the marketplace by the public. . . . "Public service" is about greed for power, which is far more dangerous than greed for wealth. . . . It is power over other people—and it is insatiable.[6]

Many people also despise the organizations through which public services so often operate. To a great extent, most civil servants function (or some would say hide) in traditional bureaucracies. The bureaucratic model is the creation of German sociologist Max Weber. Although public administration and public administrators have been attempting to substitute more modern and human organizational models, by and large such efforts have not been successful. The bureaucratic model has not disappeared; in many agencies of government, it is alive and well. Public administrators, too, often claim that it is this bureaucratic model that restricts their efforts to serve the public.

Max Weber considered the bureaucratic model the best way to run a government. It has the following general characteristics:

1. It has a fixed hierarchy.
2. It enables agencies to organize official functions according to technical rules.
3. The rules are in writing and contained in files.
4. Organizations are staffed by salaried civil servants selected on the basis of merit.
5. The organization operates impersonally on the basis of secrecy and security.

It is apparent that these circumstances provide the rationale for labeling public servants as impersonal creatures or "faceless functionaries." Indeed, many public servants behave as uninterested and impersonal agents, and have little consideration for the public good, as Sowell points out. Some use the rules of bureaucracy either not to do the job well or not to do it at all. However, regardless of the rigidity of the bureaucratic model, rules exist to ensure that employees do the job. If public servants claim that the rules prevent them from doing the job, a little imagination and ingenuity can enable them to find a way of doing it without necessarily breaking the rules. It is probably true that the public may never love public servants, but blaming the system is not always a legitimate excuse for poor or no performance.

The rules and regulations that govern the bureaucratic model are assumed to be in accordance with law, and therefore ultimately based on natural law. But this is a presumption. If they are not, there is no obligation to follow them. In fact, there is a duty not to obey. Likewise, the orders of superiors must be considered legitimate or in accordance with laws, rules and regulations. This is a question of fact; there is no obligation to obey an illegal or immoral order. Public servants are not robots. And to use the excuse of "I was just doing my job" or "I was just obeying orders" is reminiscent of excuses made regarding the Holocaust or My Lai incident during the Vietnam War. When it is certain that a superior is asking a subordinate to do something illegal or unethical, the subordinate has a corresponding duty not to obey. When a subordinate knows for certain that unethical conduct—whether waste, fraud, abuse or some other act—is occurring, there is a corresponding duty to take action. This may be risky, and it may cost a person the job, but if the employee is to serve the common good and uphold the oath of public office, it may be unethical not to act. Consequently, a public servant reflects upon and weighs the situation to determine what is real, certain and obligatory. Whistleblowing is always risky, but acting on only a hunch may also be unethical.

In summary, there is an ethical duty to obey legitimate laws, rules, regulations and orders, but there is also a duty to disobey those that are not legal or ethical. Sometimes there is ignorance or doubt, but the principles applying to vincible ignorance discussed in chapter 4 can help to resolve such conflicts. Reflection, consultation and weighing of all factors are an important part of the ethical process.

The Right to Unionize and to Strike

Earlier discussion in this chapter focused on people's right to join unions and to strike under certain conditions. How does this apply to public workers? Public employees are citizens first and have the right to work.

As workers, they have a right to form associations or unions, although there are some who think they should not do so. The right to form an association or join a union may be helpful in terms of collective bargaining or improving work conditions. But the threat of using the ultimate weapon—the strike—often seems to have the most leverage in negotiation transactions. Do public employees forfeit the right to strike by becoming public servants? Former President Reagan thought they do. In the early 1980s, he fired the striking members of the air traffic controllers' union on grounds that they did not have or had forfeited their right to strike by becoming members of the civil service.

The common good is often severely hurt by public strikes. When police, public health officials, fire personnel, teachers or air controllers strike, several aspects of the public welfare are affected. In the case of police, protection of the citizens is at stake. When air traffic controllers strike, the safety of air travelers as well as the public in general may be in jeopardy.

A strike is a means to an end. The end may be to obtain better wages or working conditions or both. Does this end justify means that place the public in danger? Those who claim that public employees do not have the right to strike argue that the end does not justify the means, and public employees forfeit the right to strike. Others maintain that public employees do have the right to strike. They say that the right to unionize is a natural right, and that part of the arsenal of unionization is the right to strike. They feel public employees do not forfeit the right to strike just by taking an oath of office.

If public employees strike, the strike may be ethical provided it follows the conditions outlined earlier in this chapter. But a state that deprives public employees of the right to strike is usurping authority and acting unethically. Let us examine why.

It is true that all strikes involve hardships and inconveniences. It is also true that the public or common good is more important than the private good. If public employees voluntarily give up the right to strike, such forfeiture appears to be ethical. The fact that a person has a right does not mean that he or she must use it. But if the state, in the name of the common good, compels public employees to give up their right to strike, it sets a dangerous precedent. What other rights may the state subsequently take away?

This issue represents a clash between the public servants' rights and the rights of citizens. Normally, the higher right—the right of the citizens, or the common good—should prevail. But public employees sometimes do strike, and in doing so, they should ensure that the public welfare is safeguarded. Is it ethical, then, for public employees to strike? The teleologist may have the best answer, after having reflected on the circumstances involved. The deontologist may decide either way. And so in practice, the public employee is free to decide between either course of action without being accused of unethical conduct.

The State and Religion

The First Amendment to the U.S. Constitution calls for a separation between church and state. This arrangement seems to work well. The United States is a pluralist society, with different ethnic groups and diverse churches and religions. It would be difficult to maintain peace and harmony if the state showed preference for one religion over another. Over the centuries, countries with state religions have experienced great conflicts and wars over religion.

There are, however, some people in the United States who disapprove of the separation of church and state. Some, including former Presidents Reagan and Bush, favor prayers in public schools. Others advocate the teaching of morals and values in the public schools. They see moral decay in America and feel it results from this separation of church and state. Some people who are critical of state involvement in the private business sector nevertheless are sympathetic toward state involvement in religious issues. On the other hand, organizations such as the American Civil Liberties Union are adamant that, regardless of any negative consequences, the Constitution's present arrangement prevents greater tragedies and must not be tampered with.

It is true that the state exists for the common good and the welfare of all its citizens. That means that the state should ensure freedom of—and perhaps freedom from—religion. But beyond that, it is my opinion that the state has no business being involved in teaching, promoting or conducting religious activities of any kind. It is not the state's business, nor does the state have the competency to engage in these activities. Churches exist for this purpose and are quite capable of fulfilling that role. The public school is not the proper forum for teaching morals and values. And the state would be compromising its position if it selected a particular set of morals and values to placate only some citizens.

Capital Punishment

Chapter 8 discussed murder, euthanasia and abortion as ethical issues for the individual. Likewise, the state has the duty to protect human life.

Indeed, protection of human life is one of the chief reasons for the existence of the state.

So how does capital punishment fit into the picture? As opposed to the abortion question—when does life begin?—or the euthanasia issue—when does life end?—we know with certainty that we are dealing with a real human life. The state is the protector of human life. Does the state ever have the right to take the life of a person?

The U.S. Supreme Court has vacillated on this issue, ruling in 1972 that capital punishment was unconstitutional and presumably contrary to natural law, then subsequently that it is constitutional. States have also wrestled with this issue. Those who maintain that capital punishment is constitutional, legal and ethical say that for certain crimes, particularly murder, the state can take a life. They argue that the criminal has forfeited his or her right to life by committing a heinous crime. Furthermore, they say capital punishment serves as the strongest deterrent to would-be criminals. These arguments are not new and have not changed much in the past half a century.[7]

Others, however, maintain that capital punishment is a primitive idea rooted in revenge; that it does not deter; that it is too risky since judicial error is possible, and that a civilized state ought to protect, not trivialize human life.[8] Some opponents of capital punishment have focused on the failure of capital punishment to deter crime and on the cases where the state has inflicted capital punishment on innocent people. And recently, some opponents of capital punishment have shown the inconsistency and bias with which it has been applied. In some cases, having a good lawyer or a lot of money is a way to avoid capital punishment.[9]

Regardless of the arguments for and against, it is difficult to figure out how the state gets the power to engage in capital punishment. In discussing rights, chapter 7 pointed out that there are certain kinds of rights that cannot be renounced or given up. One of these is the inalienable right to life. Even in a murder case, a criminal does not have the right to give up his or her inalienable right to life. And the state cannot force a criminal to do so. Natural law is the origin of this inalienable right. So, for a state to engage in capital punishment, it is usurping a human right and to this writer, such usurpation appears to be unethical. The argument that the criminal has forfeited his or her right defies the notion that the right to life is inalienable. The end does not justify the means. There are other options open to the state in administering justice, such as life in prison without parole.[10]

And the argument that capital punishment is a deterrent is weak. Again, the end does not justify the means. In fact, the means are disproportionate to the end. For elaboration on this point, see "The Case against Capital Punishment" by Donal McNamara.[11]

The State and a Just War

The state has the duty to protect and defend its citizens from enemies both foreign and domestic. Sometimes war is the only way the state can satisfy this responsibility. War often involves killing—killing of a state's own subjects as well as the enemy. Does the state have a right to take life in war?

Some argue that the state has the right to wage war in self-defense or to defend or recapture usurped rights. Yet the means by which modern warfare is carried out often involve mass destruction and the killing of innocent people—noncombatants such as women and children. Some argue that when a country is at war, everyone including women and children may be giving moral support and therefore are combatants.

Obviously, that is not true, but the means of destruction can and often do reach innocent people. It is hard to justify the means of modern warfare as proportionate to any end. Obviously, war involves a clash—a collision of rights—and should be reviewed under these conditions.

Chapter 7 discussed the right to self-defense and provided several principles that need to be satisfied before self-defense is ethical. The principles for strikes discussed earlier in this chapter have relevance. It is possible to extend a combination of these principles to determine if war is just or not. If the principles are satisfied, the war is just and it is ethical to participate in it. In practice, however, it is difficult to determine if any particular war is just. Conscientious objectors may have the right approach in claiming that no war is just.

Ethicists have developed several principles that specifically focus on whether a war is just or not. Donald Wells points out that St. Thomas Aquinas determined only three conditions were necessary to decide if a war is just: (1) the legitimate sovereign or power must declare the war; (2) there must be a just cause; (3) those engaged in the war must have good intentions so that good actually comes from the war.[12] Wells claims that for a modern war to be just, seven conditions are needed: (1) the legitimate authority must declare the war; (2) "the seriousness of the injury inflicted on the enemy must be proportional to the damage suffered by the virtuous"; (3) "the injury to the aggressor must be real and immediate"; (4) "there must be a reasonable hope of winning the war"; (5) war must be the last resort or all peaceful means to resolve the dispute must have been tried and failed; (6) "the participants must have the right intentions"; (7) "the means used must be moral."[13] These conditions ensure that wars do not start casually, that private persons cannot commit a country's citizens to a war, that there is reasonable hope of success, and that war is only the last resort. In addition, there are conditions aimed at ensuring unnecessary cruelty and suffering are not inflicted. During the Persian Gulf War of 1991, ethicists were busy applying these principles to justify that conflict. Some of the principles were easy to apply, but others were not.

Some authors distinguish between necessary and sufficient conditions. If all the necessary conditions are fulfilled, the sufficient conditions may not be met; if that is so, the war may not be a just one. A necessary condition may exist in going to war because of the attack of an aggressor, but it may not always be a sufficient condition to wage war unless other conditions are met.[14] For example, was Saddam Hussein's attack on Kuwait a sufficient condition for waging the Persian Gulf War? Was it a necessary condition? The application of these principles to specific wars is not easy. In any war, the presumption is that all conditions have been fulfilled. But this is only a presumption, and it must be verified. Doubt about the fulfillment of their conditions also serves as an ethical basis for pacifism.[15]

SUMMARY

This chapter examined the rights of human beings as members of the family, society and the state. It focused on people's right to work and to earn just wage. It considered worker needs to form unions and the right to strike. In addition, it reviewed the basis for formation of the state and the rights and duties of public employees, including their right to form unions and to strike. Finally, it provided discussion on controversial state activities, including involvement with religion, capital punishment and war.

NOTES

1. Ellen Goodman, *Washington Post*, May 21, 1992.

2. Thomas Hobbes, *The Leviathan*, Michael Oakeshott, ed. (New York: Macmillan, 1962).

3. Jean-Jacques Rousseau, *The Social Contract and Discourse on the Origin of Inequality*, Lester G. Crocker, ed. (New York: Washington Square Press, 1967).

4. Richard J. Stillman, *Preface to Public Administration: A Search for Themes and Directions* (New York: St. Martin's, 1991), pp. 173–97.

5. Harold Gortner, Julianne Mahler, and Jeanane Nicholson, *Organization Theory: A Public Perspective* (Chicago: Dorsey Press, 1987), p. 290.

6. Thomas Sowell, "So-called 'Greed' vs. Public Service," *Washington Times*, May 17, 1992.

7. Jacques Barzun, Ernest Van Den Haag, Hugo Adam Bedau, Donal E. J. Mc-Namara, "Capital Punishment," in *Morality in the Modern World: Ethical Dimensions of Contemporary Human Problems*, Lawrence Habermehl, ed. (Encino, Calif.: Dickenson Publishers, 1976), pp. 343–77.

8. Ibid., p. 344.

9. Ibid., pp. 370–77.

10. Ibid., pp. 374–77.

11. Ibid., pp. 370–77.

12. Donald Wells, "How Much Can 'The Just War' Justify?" in *Ethics and Public Policy*, Tom L. Beauchamp, ed. (Englewood Cliffs, N.J.: Prentice-Hall, 1975), p. 181.

13. Ibid., p. 182.

14. Ibid., pp. 172–73.

15. Ibid., pp. 174–75.

CHAPTER 11

Conclusion

Chapter 1 described the current state of and need for ethics in public administration. It specifically addressed the need to look at philosophy as the root of ethics. Since philosophy uses human reason alone in trying to understand humankind, the world and the Supreme Being, ethics uses the same human reason in trying to understand what makes human actions morally right or morally wrong. Whether we follow a deontological or a teleological approach, we use human reason to develop ethical principles or reflect on the meaning of actions to determine morality. But human reason is flawed—it is limited. Therefore both approaches from a philosophical perspective are limited. Consequently, this book presents a limited amount of guidance for human beings in general and public administrators in particular.

The attempt is far from perfect. On many subjects there are divergent answers to questions—and sometimes there are no answers. But the chapters build a framework for raising questions. And as former California Governor Jerry Brown has so often said, the questions are often more important than the answers. Raising these questions offers an opportunity to consider the issues.

Some will argue that this book is little more than the creation of a civil religion such as Jean-Jacques Rousseau envisioned. A civil religion smacks of ultraliberalism and will be anathema to many, particularly conservatives. But strict adherence to philosophy does not permit going beyond human reason to explore what is ethical. This may not be acceptable to those who would add religion and theology to ethics.

Ethics is neither religion nor theology. It does not and cannot use these principles if it is to remain a true philosophical science. Therefore, it cannot arrive at all the conclusions theology and religion provide. As stated in chapter 1, religion and theology certainly can supplement the findings and principles of ethics, but they cannot be added to ethics.

The previous chapter discussed the role of the state in religion and the First Amendment to the Constitution. It pointed out how difficult it would be for the state to become involved in the teaching of religion in a pluralist society. Whose religion would the state promote without offending others? To some, this is an excuse for the state's not providing more ethical guidance. They point to the common elements in religions, suggesting that these common elements provide guidance to public administrators on what is right and wrong. But if ethics does that, it no longer is rooted in philosophy. There is also the danger that theological values will be offensive to some.

Some people canonize theology as the one, true source for ethical behavior. Such a view sees ethics as pure theology, which is a distortion of the true science of ethics. But there is not always unanimity among theologians, even of the same denomination. Moral theologians in particular have had serious disagreements on what is morally right and wrong. For example, there is no consensus on the morality of abortion among some Christian denominations, even among theologians within the same denomination. Consequently, theology is not the panacea many claim it to be.

UNCOVERED ISSUES

There are many issues, problems and behaviors this volume has not covered. Chapter 1 stated that the approach was to examine ethics in the context of philosophy and use the methodology of philosophy. The intent was to develop, by the use of human reason, certain principles that could be applied to particular human actions. It was not the intent to examine all the rights and duties of the individual, the family, society and the state, or to apply ethical principles to all of them.

There are so many issues involving ethical practices by public administrators that, if treated adquately, would fill several additional volumes. Some of these issues are waste, fraud and abuse; wiring of contracts and contract overruns; conflicts of interest; stealing and unauthorized use or abuse of government property; illegal use of government transportation systems; padding of expense accounts; selection of personnel, hiring, firing, job wiring and inflation of job performance appraisals; sexual harassment; and illegal use of government equipment, such as telephones for personal calls. Other moral issues include whistleblowing; leaking government information, and spying.

How does the public administrator determine if and when these activities are ethical? This volume has developed general principles that are applicable to some specific actions. In other cases, these principles may not be applicable or they may be difficult to apply. The deontological perspective is that public administrators use reason and conscience, and that they are generally quite capable of applying general principles to specific actions. Teleological theory calls for mulling over the issues, reflecting on the meaning and significance of particular actions and making a moral judgment on each action.

PERSONAL RESPONSIBILITY

Sometimes people—including public administrators—are more comfortable having someone else decide what is right and wrong. But this attitude is reneging on personal responsibility, which is the key to ethics in practice.

In our society, people are reluctant to take personal responsibility for their actions. It is easier to find a scapegoat. This mind-set is blatant in all areas of government. It is much easier to blame anybody and everybody else when things go wrong than to assume personal responsibility for one's own actions, policies and decisions.

Former President Reagan was a master at shifting blame—blame for the poor state of the U.S. economy or the lack of military preparedness, for instance. Previous Democratic administrations, and President Carter in particular, were his scapegoats. He also blamed the Democrats for the huge deficit that was actually incurred during his administration. Following in the same vein, the initial reaction from President Bush to the Los Angeles riots in May 1992 focused blame on social programs developed by the Democrats, and those of the Great Society of President Lyndon Johnson. With that kind of action coming from the highest level of government, it should be no surprise that failure to take personal responsibility trickles down through the bureaucracy.

Some blame the bureaucratic model as conducive to shirking responsibility. Its impersonal characteristics make it easy to "pass the buck." Its culture and style also offer a haven for buck passing. People in the bureaucracy communicate via the passive voice; for example, common language is "it was decided" or "the decision was made." This way it is difficult to find out what this faceless "it" is or who made the decision.

Government often offers training courses to improve writing, and especially to change bureaucratic writing styles, but the effects are short term. The system is to some extent part of the problem, but is not the entire problem.

The purpose of the system is not only to get things done right but also to do the right things. A system is what its members make it. If the members are rotten, they will have little trouble corrupting the system. Those who blame the system for everything often have the opportunity to change or improve the system, but often invoke another often-used principle, "Don't rock the boat." And so public servants often shirk responsibility.

Terry Cooper's book *The Responsible Administrator* illustrates how public administrators must take responsibility for their actions. The example of Captain Asoh cited in chapter 1 of this book also relates to this issue. It is much easier to blame the system or some other person for mistakes, so as to cover up your own shortcomings and errors. These tactics, however, are not ethically correct. You may succeed in transferring blame for your own negligence and irresponsible behavior, thus avoiding personal embarrassment and perhaps shame, but it is unethical unless you have a certain conscience as defined in chapter 6 about the morality of your actions. Ultimately, people see personal responsibility in a manner similar to how they view human nature.

If we follow the philosophy of people such as St. Augustine, Thomas Hobbes, Frederick Taylor and Hans Morgenthau, it is clear that people are evil and cannot help but sin. Morgenthau sums up this philosophy by saying that "whenever we act with reference to fellow men, we must sin."[1] The best we can hope for is that we do not sin as much. On the other hand, the philosophy of St. Thomas Aquinas and John Locke sees people as basically good. Locke saw people as born morally neutral (*tabula rasa*), although he admitted that a few people may be born morally evil. The essential difference between good and evil people, according to Locke, is the education provided by parents.

It is very difficult to reconcile these two views of human nature. Public administrators are people, and share the same human nature. If Hobbes's pessimistic view prevails, there is not much we can do except to try to sin less. This seems to advocate abdication of personal responsibility: we cannot help being bad, therefore we are not responsible. If the more optimistic view of Locke prevails, there is some hope for improvement in assuming personal responsibility. But when we witness all the crimes committed and the number of courts, judges, prosecutors and jails we must have for law and order, we must wonder if Lockean philosophy is correct. We may wonder, too, if it does not help to condone the abdication of personal responsibility. Thomas Morgan and Ronald Rotunda have provided an excellent analysis of the professional responsibility for members of the legal profession. They ground their approach in moral philosophy or ethics,[2] and their efforts provide a solid foundation for assuming personal responsibility for actions in all professions.

In a U.S. society that the Bush administration saw as rotten and bereft of moral values, it is difficult to promote the notion of personal responsibility. In San Francisco on May 19, 1992, Vice President Quayle said: "The lawless anarchy [involved in the Los Angeles riots] which we saw is directly related to the breaking of the family structure, personal responsibility, and social order in too many areas of our society. . . . I know it is not fashionable to talk about moral values, but we need to do it." The *Washington Post* comments following Quayle's speech were: "The vice president linked the riots to the crumbling of the traditional family and personal morality, and said other culprits include broken homes, high school dropouts, drug addicts and single mothers. . . ."[3] In an effort to protect the policies of former President Reagan, Quayle placed blame on the rioters and on the social programs of the 1960s and 1970s. With people of the stature of the vice president failing to take responsibility, it should be no surprise that other people—including rioters and indeed public administrators—should do the same.

Terms such as *morality* and *values* raise additional concerns. What these terms connote to citizens is unclear. To some, values are only good habits or virtues and exclude bad habits or vices. But not everyone agrees on what is a good or a bad habit. Neither is it clear if a code of moral values exists and if so, whose it is. In practice, such words have little meaning because nobody has defined them. It is simply empty rhetoric. And these tactics provide no real example for public administrators. The key to ethical responsibility is not knowledge of laws, rules, regulations or U.S. Supreme Court decisions, but a willingness to explore and assume personal responsibility for doing the right thing. Until public administrators have a commitment to assuming personal responsibility, all that is written on ethics for public administrators is pure rhetoric.

THE DEONTOLOGICAL AND TELEOLOGICAL APPROACHES REVISITED

Deontological theory provides objective laws, rules, standards or criteria to enable public administrators to determine what is right and what is wrong. In themselves, however, these laws or criteria do not ensure that public administrators—or anyone else, for that matter—will act accordingly. This is equivalent to stating, in philosophical terminology, that laws, rules, regulations, criteria for morality or U.S. Supreme Court decisions provide merely speculative knowledge. This is knowledge for the sake of knowledge—in contrast to practical knowledge, or knowledge with a view to practice. The latter should be the goal of ethics.

The criteria for determining morality are helpful, but there are flaws. If public administrators are invincibly ignorant of these criteria, they are not responsible for their resulting actions. If they do know the relevant criteria but decide not to act accordingly or shift responsibility, they are not assuming responsibility. Speculative knowledge is no guarantee of ethical actions.

There are far too many laws, rules, regulations and Supreme Court opinions to expect public administrators to know all of them. While chapter 6 focused on laws, rules and regulations as reasonable ordinances developed and promulgated for the common good by a lawful authority, some of these are not reasonable nor are they for the common good. Discussion also focused on the duration of a law or rule. Frequently, laws remain on the books long after they have become obsolete. In addition, there are some laws and rules honored more in their breach than in their observance. When these situations occur, nobody is required to obey the law, and it is time to change it. Obsolete laws or rules sometimes remain "on the books" so that the ruler, the superior, can apply them at will, but this is not in accordance with the nature of law. A person may be perfectly ethical in not abiding by such silly principles.

The fact that there are so many laws and rules, and that it would be difficult to know all of them, makes the teleological approach to ethics easier and more practical. We share our human nature. We have intellects and free wills. We have consciences. We know by nature that certain things are right or wrong. We do not need an exhaustive list of actions branded as right and wrong. We have a sense of what is right and what is wrong after we experience an action or consider the meaning of our own or another's action. We have the capacity to reflect on, or assess the nature, circumstances and purpose of a particular action. We compare it with other actions, look at alternative courses of action and make a judgment about this activity.

This is a process of ethical decision making. It is the teleological approach. It may be subjective, but it is a personal process that involves the steps described above. In the final analysis, this process may be the best and easiest to determine what is right or wrong. The judgment could go either way, but conscience has the capacity of judging. Likewise, the teleological approach is more conducive to generating a sense of personal responsibility.

NOTES

1. Hans J. Morgenthau, *Politics Among Nations*, Fourth Edition (New York: Alfred A. Knopf, 1967), p. 39.

2. Thomas D. Morgan and Ronald D. Rotunda, *Professional Responsibility*, Third Edition (Mineola, N.Y.: Foundation Press, 1984).

3. *Washington Post*, May 20, 1992.

EDUARDO U. RODRIGUEZ CALVET
Relacionador Industrial

Selected Bibliography

American Society for Public Administration. *Code of Ethics and Implementation Guidelines.* Washington, D.C.: American Society for Public Administration, 1984.

Appleby, Paul H. *Morality and Administration in Democratic Government.* Westport, Conn.: Greenwood Press, 1969.

Aristotle. *The Ethics of Aristotle,* edited by J.A.K. Thomson. London: Penguin Books, 1955.

Baier, Kurt. *The Moral Point of View: A Rational Basis of Ethics.* Ithaca, N.Y.: Cornell University Press, 1958.

Bailey, Stephen K. "Ethics and the Public Service." *Public Administration Review* 23 (1964): 234–43.

Barrett, Laurence I. "Ethics: Sounds of the Righteous Brothers." *Time,* May 25, 1987, p. 21.

Barzun, Jacques et al. "Capital Punishment." In *Morality in the Modern World: Ethical Dimensions of Contemporary Problems,* edited by Lawrence Habermehl. Encino, Calif.: Dickenson Publishers, 1976.

Bayles, Michael D. *Professional Ethics,* 2nd ed. Belmont, Calif.: Wadsworth, 1989.

Beauchamp, Tom L., ed. *Ethics and Public Policy.* Englewood Cliffs, N.J.: Prentice-Hall, 1975.

Bellavita, Christopher, ed. *How Public Organizations Work: Learning from Experience.* New York: Praeger, 1990.

Bentham, Jeremy. *The Principles of Morals and Legislation.* New York: Hofner Press, 1948.

Bergerson, Peter. *Ethics and Public Policy: An Annotated Bibliography.* New York: Garland Publishing, 1988.

Blake, Eugene Carson. "Should the Code of Ethics in Public Life Be Absolute or Relative?" *Annals of the American Academy of Political and Social Science* 363 (January 1966): 4–11.

Bok, Sissela. *Lying: Moral Choices in Public and Private Life*. New York: Random House, 1978.

———. *Secrets*. New York: Vintage, 1984.

Boling, T. Edwin. "Organizational Ethics: Rules, Creativity, and Idealism." In *Management Handbook for Public Administration*, edited by John W. Sutherland. New York: Van Nostrand Reinhold, 1978.

Bolles, Blair. "Correctives for Dishonest and Unfair Public Administrators." *Annals of the American Academy of Political and Social Sciences* 363 (January 1966): 23–27.

Bowen, Ezra. "Ethics: Looking to its Roots." *Time*, May 25, 1987, pp. 26–29.

Bowman, James S. "Whistle Blowing: Literature and Resource Materials." *Public Administration Review* 43, no. 3 (1983): 271–76.

———. et al. *Managerial Ethics: Whistleblowing in Organizations: An Annotated Bibliography and Resource Guide*. New York: Garland Publishing, 1982.

Bradley, Paul John, ed. *The Holy Bible*, Catholic Action edition. Gustonia, N.C.: Goodwill Publishers, 1953.

Buchanan, Patrick. "The Desecration of St. Patrick's." *Washington Times*, December 18, 1989.

Buckingham, Major J. C. "A Code of Ethics." *Proceedings* (December 1989).

Burns, Chester R., ed. *Legacies in Ethics and Medicine*. New York: Science History Publications, 1977.

Burrell, Gibson, and Gareth Morgan. *Sociological Paradigms and Organizational Analysis*. Portsmouth, N.H.: Heinemann, 1985.

Callahan, Daniel. *Abortion, Law, Choice, and Morality*. New York: Macmillan, 1970.

———. et al., eds. *Applying the Humanities*. New York: Plenum Pres, 1985.

Callahan, Daniel, and Bruce Jennings, eds. *Ethics, the Social Sciences, and Policy Analysis*. New York: Plenum Press, 1983.

Callahan, Daniel, and Sissela Bok, eds. *Ethics Teaching in Higher Education*. New York: Plenum Press, 1980.

Callahan, Daniel, and H. Tristram Englehardt. *The Roots of Ethics—Science, Religion, and Values*. New York: Plenum Press, 1981.

Caplan, Arthur, and Daniel Callahan. *Ethics in Hard Times*. New York: Plenum Press, 1984.

Caplan, Arthur J. and Bruce Jennings, eds. *Darwin, Marx and Freud: Their Influence on Moral Theory*. New York: Plenum Press, 1984.

Caro, Robert. *The Power Broker: Robert Moses and the Fall of New York City*. New York: Vintage Books, 1974.

Carson, Charles R. *Managing Employee Honesty*. Los Angeles: Security World Publishing Co., 1977.

Chandler, Robert C. "The Problems of Moral Illiteracy in Professional Discourse: The Case of the State Principles of the ASPA." *American Review of Public Administration* 16 (Winter 1982): 369–86.

Connery, John. *Abortion: The Development of the Roman Catholic Perspective*. Chicago: Loyola Press, 1977.

Cooper, Terry L. *The Responsible Administrator: An Approach to Ethics for the Administrative Role*. Rev. ed. Port Washington, N.Y.: Associated Faculty Press, 1986.

Curran, Charles. "Contemporary Debate in Philosophical and Religious Ethics." *Encyclopedia of Bioethics*, edited by Warren T. Reich. New York: Free Press, 1978.

Curtis, Michael J., ed. *The Great Political Theories*. New York: Avon Books, 1961.

DeGeorge, Richard T. *Business Ethics*. 2nd ed. New York: Macmillan, 1986.

Denhardt, Katherine G. *The Ethics of Public Service: Resolving Moral Dilemmas in Public Organizations*. Westport, Conn.: Greenwood Press, 1988.

De Tocqueville, Alexis. *Democracy in America*, edited by Richard D. Heffner. New York: New American Library, 1956.

Dewey, John, and J. H. Tufts. *Ethics*. New York: Henry Holt, 1932.

Drucker, Peter F. *Management*. New York: Harper and Row, 1984.

Eckel, Malcolm W. *The Ethics of Decision Making*. New York: Morehouse-Barlow, 1968.

Erickson, Erick. *Gandhi's Truth*. New York: W. W. Norton, 1969.

Erwing, David W. *Do It My Way or You Will Be Fired*. New York: John Wiley & Sons, 1983.

"Ethics? Bah, Humbug." *Washington Post*, December 12, 1991.

Ethics Factor Handbook. Washington, D.C.: International City Management Association, 1988.

Ethics in Government Act of 1978. Public Law 95–51, as amended. 5 U.S.C. app. 201 *et seq.*

Falik, Marilyn. *Ideology and Abortion Policy Politics*. New York: Praeger, 1983.

Fisher, F. *Politics, Values and Public Policy*. Boulder, Colo.: Westview, 1982.

Fleishman, Joel et al. *Public Duties: The Moral Obligations of Government Officials*. Cambridge, Mass.: Harvard University Press, 1981.

Fletcher, Joseph. "Ethics and Euthanasia." In *Morality in the Modern World*, edited by Lawrence Habermehl. Encino, Calif.: Dickenson Publishing Company, 1976.

——— . *Situation Ethics: The New Morality*. New York: Westminster Press, 1966.

Flew, Anthony. "The Principle of Euthanasia." In *Morality in the Modern World*, edited by Lawrence Habermehl. Encino, Calif.: Dickenson Publishing Company, 1976.

Foot, Philippa. *Virtues and Vices and Other Essays in Moral Philosophy*. Berkeley, Calif.: University of California Press, 1978.

Frankena, William K. *Ethics*. 2nd ed. Englewood Cliffs, N.J.: Prentice-Hall, 1973.

French, Peter A. *Ethics in Government*. Englewood Cliffs, N.J.: Prentice-Hall, 1983.

Garfinckel, H. *Studies in Ethnomethodology*. London: Prentice-Hall, 1967.

Gathrop, Louis C. *Public Sector Management Systems, and Ethics*. Bloomington, Ind.: Indiana University Press, 1984.

Gerwirth, Alan. *Reason and Morality*. Chicago: Universtiy of Chicago Press, 1978.

Gilligan, C. *In a Different Voice: Psychological Theory and Women's Development*. Cambridge, Mass.: Harvard University Press, 1982.

Golembiewski, Robert T. *Men, Management and Morality: Toward a New Organizational Ethic*. New York: McGraw-Hill, 1965.

Gorman, Charles. "Ethics: A Balancing Act of Life and Death." *Time*, February 1, 1988.

Gibson, Winter. *Elements for a Social Ethic: The Role of Social Sciences in Public Policy*. New York: Macmillan, 1966.

Goodman, Ellen. *Washington Post*, May 21, 1992.

Gortner, Harold F. *Ethics for Public Managers*. New York: Praeger, 1991.

——— . et al. *Organization Theory: A Public Perspective*. Chicago: Dorsey Press, 1987.

Goulder, A. W. *Wildcat Strike*. New York: Harper and Row, 1965.

Gustafson, James M. *Theology and Christian Ethics*. Philadelphia: United Church Press, 1974.

Guttman, Amy, and Dennis Thompson. *Ethics and Politics*. Chicago: Nelson-Hall, 1984.

Habermehl, Lawrence, ed. *Morality in the Modern World*. Encino, Calif.: Dickenson Publishing Company, 1976.

Hagberg, Janet. *Real Power*. New York: Winston Press, 1986.

Hampshire, Stuart. *Morality and Conflict*. Cambridge, Mass.: Harvard University Press, 1983.

Harmon, Michael. *Action Theory for Public Administration*. New York: Longman, 1981.

Harrison, Beverly. *Our Right to Choose*. Boston: Beacon Press, 1983.

Hart, D. K. "Social Equity, Justice, and the Equitable Administrator." *Public Administration Review* 3, no. 1 (January-February, 1974): 3–10.

Hastings Center. *The Ethics of Legislative Life*. Hastings-on-Hudson, N.Y.: Plenum Press, 1985.

Hellegers, Andre E. "Abortion." In *Encyclopedia of Bioethics*, edited by Warren T. Reich. New York: Free Press, 1978.

Hobbes, Thomas. *The Leviathan*, edited by Michael Oakeshott. New York: Macmillan, 1962.

Jackall, Robert. *Moral Mazes: The World of Corporate Managers*. New York: Oxford University Press, 1988.

Jennings, Bruce, and Daniel Callahan, eds. *Representation and Responsibility: Exploring Legislative Ethics*. New York: Plenum Press, 1985.

Jones, W. T. *Approaches to Ethics: Representative Selections from Classical Times to the Present*. 3rd ed. New York: McGraw-Hill, 1977.

Jonsen, Albert R., and Andre E. Hellegers. "Conceptual Foundations for an Ethics of Medical Care." In *Ethics for Health Care*, edited by Laurence R. Tancredi. Washington, D.C.: National Academy of Sciences, 1974.

Kaplan, Abraham. *American Ethics and Public Policy*. 1963. Reprint. Westport, Conn.: Greenwood Press, 1980.

Kelbley, Charles. "Abortion: Agreeing to Disagree." *Newsweek*, December 13, 1985.

Kernaghan, Kenneth, and O. P. Dwivedi, eds. *Ethics in the Public Service: Comparative Perspectives*. Brussels: International Institute of Administrative Sciences, 1983.

Kimbrough, Robert T. *Summary of American Law*. San Francisco: Bancroft-Whitney, 1974.

Koepp, Stephen. "Having It All, Then Throwing It Away." *Time*, May 25, 1987, pp. 22–23.

Lakoff, George, and Mark Johnson. *Metaphors We Live By*. Chicago: Chicago University Press, 1980.

Lane, Robert E. *Political Ideology: Why the American Common Man Believes What He Believes*. New York: Free Press, 1962.

Laney, James T. "Moralizing the Professions: Commitment to the Public Interest." *Vital Speeches of the Day* 51 (June 1, 1985): 501–503.

Leys, Wayne A. R. *Ethics and Social Policy*. New York: Prentice-Hall, 1941.

Lilla, Mark. "Ethos, 'Ethics,' and Public Service." *Public Interest* 63 (Spring 1981).

Locke, John. *Two Treatises of Government*, edited by Peter Laslett. New York: Cambridge University Press, 1960.

Losito, William F. "Is Ethical Conduct Among Professionals Attainable?" *USA Today Magazine*, 1983, pp. 22–24.

Luckman, T. *The Social Construction of Reality*. New York: Doubleday, 1966.

Machiavelli, Niccolo. *The Prince*, translated by George Bull. New York: Penguin Books, 1981.

MacIntyre, Alisdair. *After Virtue*. 2nd ed. Notre Dame: Notre Dame University Press, 1984.

———. *A Short History of Ethics*. New York: Collier, 1966.

Manning, Frank V. *Managerial Dilemmas and Executive Growth*. Reston, Va.: Reston Publishing Co., 1981.

Martins, Herman, and Patrick J. Hennigan. *Applying Professional Standards and Ethics in the Eighties: A Workbook and Study Guide for Public Administrators*. Washington, D.C.: American Society for Public Administration, 1982.

Mattingly, Kimberly A. "The Ethical Noose." *Government Executive*, February 1989.

Mayer, Richard, and Harmon, Michael. "Teaching Moral Education in Public Administration." *Southern Review of Public Administration* 6, no. 2 (Summer 1982).

McCormick, Richard A. *How Brave a New World? Dilemmas in Bioethics*. Garden City, N.Y.: Doubleday, 1981.

McKeegan, Michele. *Abortion Politics: Mutiny in the Ranks of the Right*. New York: Free Press, 1992.

McSwain, Cynthia J., and White, Orion F., Jr. "The Case for Lying, Cheating, and Stealing—Personal Development as Ethical Guidance for Managers." *Administration and Society* 18, no. 4 (February 1987).

Means, Cyril L. *The Ethical Imperative*. Garden City, N.Y.: Anchor Books, 1970.

Milgram, Stanley. *Obedience to Authority*. New York: Harper and Row, 1974.

Mitchell, Greg. "Blowing the Whistle." *Washington Post Magazine*, August 12, 1979, pp. 12–19.

Mohr, James C. *Abortion in America: The Origins and Evolution of National Policy 1800–1900*. New York: Oxford University Press, 1978.

Moore, W. John. "The Office of Government Ethics: Vigilant Watchdog or Toothless Terrier." *Government Executive*, October 1987, pp. 22–25.

Morgan, Thomas, and Ronald D. Rotunda. *Professional Responsibility*. 3rd ed. Mineola, N.Y.: Foundation Press, 1984.

Morgenthau, Hans J. *Politics Among Nations*. 4th ed. New York: Alfred A. Knopf, 1967.

Morrow, Lance. "Charging up Capital Hill: How Oliver North Captured the Imagination of America." *Time*, July 20, 1987, pp. 12–15.

Nader, Ralph, Peter J. Parkas, and Kate Blackwell, eds. *Whistle Blowing: The Report of the Conference on Professional Responsibility*. New York: Grossman Publishers, 1972.

Niebuhr, Reinhold. *Moral Man and Immoral Society: A Study of Ethics and Politics*. 1932. Reprint. New York: Scribners, 1960.

Noonan, John T., Jr. *The Morality of Abortion: Legal and Historical Perspectives*. Cambridge, Mass.: Harvard University Press, 1970.

———. *A Private Choice*. New York: Free Press, 1979.

Office of Government Ethics. *How to Keep out of Trouble*. Washington, D.C.: Government Printing Office, 1986.

Pegis, Anton C., ed. *Basic Writings of Saint Thomas Aquinas*. New York: Random House, 1945.

Peter, Charlers. *How Washington Really Works*. Reading, Mass.: Addison Wesley, 1983.

Pope Leo XIII. "Rerum Novarum." In *The Papal Encyclicals*, edited by Anne Fremantle. New York: New American Library of World Literature, 1956.

Pope Pius XI. "Quadragessimo Anno." In *The Papal Encyclicals*, edited by Anne Fremantle. New York: New American Library of World Literature, 1956.

Pound, Roscoe. *An Introduction to the Philosophy of Law*. New Haven, Conn.: Yale University Press, 1954.

Powers, Charles W., and David Vogel. *Ethics in the Education of Business Managers*. Hastings-on-Hudson, N.Y.: Hastings Center, 1983.

Ramsey, Paul. *Ethics at the Edges of Life*. New Haven, Conn.: Yale University Press, 1978.

Raspberry, William. "Ethics Without Virtue." *Washington Post*, December 16, 1991.

Rawls, J. *Theory of Justice*. Cambridge, Mass.: Harvard University Press, 1971.

Reagan, Ronald. *Abortion and the Conscience of the Nation*. New York: Thomas Nelson, 1984.

Reich, Warren T., ed. *Encyclopedia of Bioethics*. New York: Free Press, 1978.

Richter, William L. et al. *Combatting Corruption: Encouraging Ethics: A Sourcebook for Public Service Ethics*. Washington, D.C.: American Society for Public Administration, 1990.

Rohr, John A. *Ethics for Bureaucrats*. New York: Marcel Decker, 1978.

Rosmini, Antonio. *The Origin of Ideas*. London: Tench and Company, 1883.

Rousseau, Jean-Jacques. *The Social Contract and Discourse on the Origin of Inequality*, edited by Lester G. Crocker. New York: Washington Square Press, 1967.

Sabine, George H., and Thomas L. Thorson. *A History of Political Theory*. 4th ed. Hinsdale, Ill.: Dryden Press, 1973.

Sanders, Alain L. "Ethics: Whose Right to Die?" *Time*, December 11, 1989, p. 80.

Sartre, J. P. *Being and Nothingness*. Secaucus, N.J.: Citadel, 1965.

Shapiro, Walter. "Ethics: What's Wrong." *Time*, May 25, 1987, pp. 14–17.

Sheeran, Patrick J. *Women, Society, the State and Abortion: A Structuralist Analysis*. New York: Praeger, 1987.

Singer, Marcus. *Generalization in Ethics*. New York: Alfred A. Knopf, 1961.

Sittomer, Curtis J. "Morals and Public Money." *Christian Science Monitor*, November 27, 1987.

Smith, Adam. *The Theory of Moral Sentiments*, edited by D. D. Raphael and A. L. Mackie. Oxford, England: Clarendon Press, 1976.

Southard, Samuel. *Ethics for Executives*. New York: Cornerstone Library, 1977.

Sowell, Thomas. "So-called 'Greed' vs. Public Service." *Washington Times*, May 17, 1992.

Spence, Larry D. "Moral Judgment and Bureaucracy." In *Moral Development and Politics*, edited by W. Wilson and Gordon J. Schochet. New York: Praeger, 1980.

Stengel, Richard. "Morality Among the Supply-Siders." *Time*, May 25, 1987, pp. 18–20.

Stillman, Richard J. *Preface to Public Administration: A Search for Themes and Direction*. New York: St. Martin's, 1991.

Stromberg, Peter et al. *The Teaching of Ethics in the Military*. Hastings-on-Hudson, N.Y.: Hastings Center, 1982.

Struckmeyer, Frederick R. "The 'Just War' and the Right of Self-Defense." In *Morality in the Modern World*, edited by Lawrence Habermehl. Encino, Calif.: Dickenson Publishing Company, 1976.

Sutherland, John W. *Management Handbook for Public Administration*. New York: Van Nostrand Reinhold, 1978.

Thompson, Dennis. "The Possibility of Administrative Ethics." *Public Administration Review* 45, no. 5 (1985): 555–61.

Thomson, J.A.K., ed. *The Ethics of Aristotle*. London: Penguin Books, 1955.

Toulmin, Stephen E. *An Examination of the Place of Ethics*. Cambridge, England: Cambridge University Press, 1950.

Tower, John et al. *Report of the President's Special Review Board*. Washington, D.C.: Government Printing Office, 1987.

Tribe, Lawrence H. *Abortion: The Clash of Absolutes*. New York: W. W. Norton, 1990.

Turelson, J. A. *Blowing the Whistle on Systematic Corruption*. Ph.D. Dissertation, University of Southern California.

U.S. Department of Health and Human Services. *Standards of Conduct*. Washington, D.C.: Government Printing Office, 1981.

———. *Standards of Conduct in Brief: A Handbook for Employees of the Department of Health and Human Services*. Personnel Pamphlet Series No. 6. Washington, D.C.: Government Printing Office.

Wakefield, Susan. "Ethics and the Public Service: A Case for Individual Responsibility." *Public Administration Review* (November-December 1976): 661–66.

Weisband, Edward, and Thomas M. Frank. *Resignation in Protest: Political and Ethical Choices Between Loyalty to Team and Loyalty to Conscience in American Public Life*. New York: Grossman Publishers, 1975.

Wells, Donald. "How Much Can 'The Just War' Justify?" In *Ethics and Public Policy*, edited by Tom L. Beauchamp. Englewood Cliffs, N.J.: Prentice-Hall, 1975.

Westin, Alan F., Henry I. Kurtz, and Albert Robbins, eds. *Whistle Blowing: Loyalty and Dissent in the Corporation*. New York: McGraw-Hill, 1981.

"Whatever Happened to Ethics?" *Time*, May 25, 1987, pp. 14–29.

Willbern, Harold L. "Types and Levels of Public Morality." *Public Administration Review* 44, no. 2 (1984): 102–108.

Wilson, Richard W., and Gordon J. Schochet, eds. *Moral Development and Politics*. New York: Praeger, 1980.

Wood, P. C. "Ethics in Government as a Problem of Executive Management." *Public Administration Review* 40 (1955).

Zelermyer, William. *Legal Reasoning: The Evolutionary Process of Law*. Englewood Cliffs, N.J.: Prentice-Hall, 1960.

Index

About the Author

PATRICK J. SHEERAN holds a Doctorate in Public Administration and a Masters in International Relations from the University of Southern California. Sheeran is a former Catholic priest and has taught various graduate courses in public administration, including ethics, at the University of Southern California, George Mason University, and Shenandoah University. He is the author of *Women, Society, the State and Abortion: A Structuralist Analysis* (Praeger, 1987).

EDUARDO U. RODRIGUEZ G U V??
al Relacionador Industrial